T0323917

Cambridge Elements ≡

Elements in Global Development Studies
edited by
Peter Ho
Zhejiang University
Servaas Storm
Delft University of Technology

EMIGRATION STATES

Migration-Development Policymaking in the Asia-Pacific

Matt Withers
Australian National University

CAMBRIDGE
UNIVERSITY PRESS

Shaftesbury Road, Cambridge CB2 8EA, United Kingdom

One Liberty Plaza, 20th Floor, New York, NY 10006, USA

477 Williamstown Road, Port Melbourne, VIC 3207, Australia

314–321, 3rd Floor, Plot 3, Splendor Forum, Jasola District Centre, New Delhi – 110025, India

103 Penang Road, #05–06/07, Visioncrest Commercial, Singapore 238467

Cambridge University Press is part of Cambridge University Press & Assessment, a department of the University of Cambridge.

We share the University's mission to contribute to society through the pursuit of education, learning and research at the highest international levels of excellence.

www.cambridge.org
Information on this title: www.cambridge.org/9781009565196

DOI: 10.1017/9781009318716

First published 2024

A catalogue record for this publication is available from the British Library

ISBN 978-1-009-56519-6 Hardback
ISBN 978-1-009-31874-7 Paperback
ISSN 2634-0313 (online)
ISSN 2634-0305 (print)

Emigration States

Migration-Development Policymaking in the Asia-Pacific

Elements in Global Development Studies

DOI: 10.1017/9781009318716
First published online: December 2024

Matt Withers
Australian National University

Author for correspondence: Matt Withers, matt.withers@anu.edu.au

Abstract: Guestworker migration has become an increasingly prominent feature within the economic landscape of the Asia-Pacific. Longstanding regional disparities have underscored the emergence of fragile remittance economies where a structural reliance on labour-export has offered an unsustainable 'fix' for stubborn developmental challenges. Combining political-economic and Foucauldian frames of analysis, this Element reconciles the macroeconomic contradictions of remittance economies with the political logics bound up in emigration policymaking, contending that new modalities of governance have emerged in the transition from developmental to emigration states. Comparing the policy histories of four diverse remittance economies in the region – Myanmar, the Philippines, Samoa, and Sri Lanka – it frames emigration policies as complex, inward-facing interventions that simultaneously promote and constrain mobility to address counterpoised economic and political pressures. Important variations are explored though the example of gendered migration bans, whereby emigration states have situated women's bodies as sites for resolving contextually specific social tensions accompanying labour export.

Keywords: emigration states, remittance economies, temporary labour migration, migration bans, migration governance

ISBNs: 9781009565196 (HB), 9781009318747 (PB), 9781009318716 (OC)
ISSNs: 2634-0313 (online), 2634-0305 (print)

Contents

Introduction: Remittance Economies and Emigration States

International temporary labour migration and the remittances it generates have become increasingly prominent features within the economic landscape of the Asia-Pacific region. For countries with limited viable livelihood opportunities, foreign employment can act as a 'safety valve' for local unemployment and accompanying political unrest (Wickramasekara 2016), while simultaneously encouraging remittance transfers with the potential to provide poverty-clearing income to migrant households and much-needed foreign exchange earnings to ease macroeconomic constraints (Ratha & Mohapatra 2013). In 2019, just prior to the onset of the COVID-19 pandemic, migrant workers' private income transfers to low- and middle-income countries eclipsed foreign direct investment (FDI) for the first time, becoming the single largest source of capital flowing into emerging economies (World Bank 2020). Yet, despite broad enthusiasm for the prospect of migration-led development among global and regional policymakers, several major labour-sending states have become reliant on temporary labour migration and remittances in a manner that appears detrimental to transformative[1] or sustainable[2] development outcomes. These 'remittance economies' typically feature structural and institutional dependencies on continued foreign employment that can ingrain exploitative labour relations and stymie local development initiatives as increasing inflows of remittances are required to maintain macroeconomic stability (Delgado Wise 2009; Phillips 2009; Withers 2019b). Such scenarios are readily identifiable across the Asia-Pacific region, challenging the enduring claims of 'triple-win' migration (World Bank 2006; Wickramasekara 2011; Angenendt 2014; Bauböck & Ruhs 2022) and the general enthusiasm surrounding remittances as a source of developmental capital (Chi 2008). This critique of remittances intervenes at the very heart of the 'migration-development' debate, curbing overly optimistic expectations of the potential for remittances to drive economic growth at local and national scales (de Haas 2012; Chami *et al.* 2018). It also complicates the presumed political aims and objectives of labour-sending states that are regularly understood to be promoting 'labour export' in pursuit of economic development.

Beyond a handful of pioneering studies (Levitt & De La Dehesa 2003; Østergaard-Nielsen 2003; Oishi 2005; Yeates 2009), comparative analyses of

---

[1] Transformative development here refers to local capital formation, rather than the more radical notion of transformative development as transcending capitalist social relations (Petras 1983).

[2] Sustainable development minimally refers to meeting minimum standards of equitable and inclusive wellbeing within a threshold of ecological and planetary boundaries, but extends to a broader interpretation relating to the social reproduction of labour power and societal relations (Collins 1991).

the policies that promote labour export and sustain remittance economies have been lacking. Academic and policymaking literature has enduringly emphasised the *immigration* policies of destination states in determining migration processes and outcomes while largely overlooking the importance of *emigration* policies (Gamlen 2014; Boucher & Gest 2015; Agarwala 2022). In the past decade, important strands of comparative migration scholarship have sought to correct this oversight, drawing attention to proliferating diaspora institutions (Gamlen 2014, 2019) and expanding typologies of migration management regimes to better account for variations within Global South contexts (Adamson & Tsourapas 2020). Gamlen (2019) casts a wide net in defining state–diaspora relations, reserving a distinct subcategory for labour export strategies, which he sees converging around an archetypal 'Filipino Model' defined by active state involvement in labour brokerage as a means of regulating political and economic stability. Adamson and Tsourapas (2020), meanwhile, identify a similar 'developmental migration state' as one of three broad permutations within Global South migration regimes, alongside 'nationalising' and 'neoliberal' variants. Both departures are useful insofar as they seek to expand the purview of comparative migration research by foregrounding emigration policies and making high-level distinctions between managing temporary labour migration and regulating other forms of cross-border population movement. Yet, in seeking to establish broad commonalities demanded by typology, they also gloss over important variations within the policymaking of emigration states. With respect to states predominantly involved in labour export, reductive 'safety valve' explanations remain largely unstirred.

Inattentiveness to the diversity of emigration policies among labour-sending states is striking in the broader context of migration studies' ongoing 'reflexive turn' (Dahinden *et al.* 2021) and the associated recentring of Southern contexts and perspectives (Crawley & Teye 2024; Fiddian-Qasmiyeh 2024). A flurry of recent comparative migration scholarship seeking to revisit Hollifield's (2004) formulation of the migration state has embraced this epistemological shift insofar as emphasising Global South immigration policies (Gazzotti, Mouthaan, & Natter 2023; Chung, Hollifield, & Tian 2023; Chung, Draudt, & Tian 2024; Klotz 2024) and emigration policies relating to postcolonial nation-building and transnational citizenship (Sadiq & Tsourapas 2021; Adamson, Chung, & Hollifield 2024), or else more radically eschewing the immigration/emigration binary altogether (Lacroix 2022; Triandafyllidou 2022). This literature has, however, continued to neglect the policy complexity of distinctive labour-sending states – particularly concerning the political and economic tensions that can arise when national development is predicated upon integration with highly exploitative foreign labour markets that undermine individual and collective rights. Natter (2024: 681) reminds us that 'migration by defin-ition cuts across questions of security, culture, economy, and rights at national and international levels, and so migration states are inevitably faced with trade-offs when developing their migration policies'. Labour-sending states are no less constrained by these considerations and likewise encounter trade-offs when designing emigration policies. Indeed, while Hollifield's (1992) 'liberal para-dox' has garnered enduring interest concerning the way immigration states balance the economic returns of migration against the political value of restrict-ive borders (Natter 2024), little consideration has been given to complex and varied ways in which emigration states might simultaneously promote and constrain labour export to achieve similar ends.

This Element addresses such oversights by combining political-economic and Foucauldian frames of analysis to examine the emigration policymaking of four distinctive labour-sending states of the Asia-Pacific region: Myanmar, the Philippines, Samoa, and Sri Lanka. Together, these country studies reveal that emigration policies are instrumental in attempting to reconcile economic objectives with an entanglement of adjacent – and sometimes countervailing – social, cultural, and political interests. Contrary to the 'safety valve' metaphor, widespread emigration is not seen to vent or stabilise political pressure so much as to create new challenges for governance as the contradictions of remittance economies become apparent at macroeconomic and household scales. Though all four countries are drawn to the prospect of 'exporting' unemployment and 'importing' remittances, as are many others in the region and globally, the promotion of temporary labour migration can also generate domestic political unrest by deepening uneven development (Ness 2023), undermining conditions of decent work (Piper, Rosewarne, & Withers 2017), and disrupting the life-making work of social reproduction (Kofman & Raghuram 2015). These broad structural changes interface with various contextually specific factors – includ-ing differing colonial histories, demographic profiles of migrant workforces, and norms and values scaffolding migration practices – resulting in heterogen-ous expressions of a more fundamental tension between the economic and political implications of labour export. Emigration consequently emerges as a complex and varied policy domain that can involve assertive state interven-tions to mediate and restrict mobility at critical junctures, as well as more diffusive exercises in governmentality (Foucault 1991) that seek to 'responsi-bilise' migrant households living on the margins of development. In exploring rich permutations among these policies – which look *inward* to domestic concerns as much as they do *outward* to foreign labour markets – I contend that emigration has become a key project through which the political legitimacy of erstwhile developmental states has been reconstructed in lieu of more transformative visions for local economies.

In short, the emergence of 'remittance economies' implies the existence of a particular type of 'emigration state'[3] with complicated (and sometimes contradictory) policymaking objectives that remain largely overlooked and undertheorised within comparative migration scholarship. In the context of the Asia-Pacific, where temporary labour migration abounds as a livelihood strategy, the political economy of the region demands to be understood as not only shaped by the immigration regimes of labour-receiving states but also – and substantially – the emigration policymaking of labour-sending states (Agarwala 2022). Analysing these varying policy logics is, therefore, an important task, both in reconciling the economic dynamics of remittance economies with the political imperatives of emigration states, but also in establishing the barriers to be overcome in pursuit of more inclusive, just, and sustainable development pathways.

Migration and Remittances in the Asia-Pacific

The Asia-Pacific is a sprawling region, spanning the breadth of Asia and Oceania while encompassing some of the most and least developed economies of either continent and, indeed, of the entire world economy. It is a political-economic expanse characterised by historical structures of uneven development and entrenched inequality, whose fault lines were hewn during intensive periods of European imperialism and are enduringly illuminated by the scale and direction of temporary labour migration flows between poorer and wealthier regions (Yeoh 2019). If for no other reason, it is perhaps these shared colonial legacies and the sheer prevalence of intraregional guestworker migration flows that lend coherence to a geopolitical construct that might otherwise appear a loose grouping of disparate countries.

West Asian economies, particularly the oil-producing Gulf Cooperation Council (GCC) member states, have long depended on the mass migration of low-wage guestworkers from South and Southeast Asia as an *in situ* 'fix' for production and social reproduction underpinning local development (Cohen 1987; Kaur 2004). The total number of temporary migrant workers in the GCC, most of whom are employed in domestic work and construction, has increased from 1.4 million in 1975 to 35 million in 2020, with those workers comprising as

---

[3] Hereafter, 'emigration state' will be used to refer to the governance of remittance economies engaged in labour-export strategies, as opposed to the broader definition prevalent in the comparative migration literature.

much as 90 per cent of the total population in Qatar and 85 per cent in the UAE (World Bank 2023). There are similar patterns of migrant labour moving into the wealthier economies of East and Southeast Asia – though with slightly greater occupational diversity (Sarkar 2017). Singapore and Hong Kong, for example, have comparable migration skill profiles to the GCC countries, and foreign workers comprise 45 per cent and 40 per cent of their respective populations (World Bank 2023); Taiwan and Malaysia also employ migrant workers in export manufacturing industries (in addition to domestic work, construction and service industries) and have a relatively lower concentration of migrant workers as a share of their total populations at 3 and 8 per cent respectively (World Bank 2023). Meanwhile, at the very fringes of the region, the two Anglospheric countries – Australia and New Zealand – both increasingly rely on guestworkers from neighbouring Pacific Island Countries (PICs) to provide low-wage labour for rural and regional labour markets whose prevailing employment standards fail to attract sufficient local workers (Campbell 2019; Petrou & Connell 2023). In each corner of the Asia-Pacific, then, key labour-intensive sectors of wealthier economies are propped up to greater or lesser degrees by reserve armies of labour originating from poorer economies.

An attendant, but no less significant, outcome of deepening transnational labour regimes across the Asia-Pacific has been the steady increase in remittance transfers to migrant workers' countries of origin. India has the largest foreign workforce in the region and receives more remittances than any other country in the world, recording $83.1 billion in private income transfers during 2019 – a sum tallying to 2.8 per cent of gross domestic product (GDP) for the same year (World Bank 2020). In this context, temporary labour migration plays out on a grand scale, providing livelihood opportunities for millions of households that, while often not the poorest of the poor, have nonetheless been excluded from the limited and highly concentrated growth industries that drive India's economy (Hill & Palit 2018). At the other end of the spectrum, the Asia-Pacific is host to numerous smaller economies with substantially higher rates of emigration per capita, where remittances make up a much larger portion of GDP. For these economies, such as Tonga and Nepal, where remittances contributed 37.6 and 27.3 per cent of GDP, respectively, in 2019 (World Bank 2020), dependency on migration is far more acute and reflects a more generalised absence of locally available livelihood opportunities within the cash economy or, indeed, viable pathways to (capitalist) development. For the small island countries of the South Pacific, where common blueprints for economic development are particularly unsuitable in the face of geographic and demographic obstacles to accumulation, the challenges associated with being a 'MIRAB' (migration, remittances, aid and bureaucracy) economy remains pertinent (Brown & Ahlburg 1999; Prasad 2003; Bertram 2006). Between these extremes are a diverse variety of countries where migration and remittances account for a more modest share of employment and GDP but remain structurally intractable – insofar as the promotion of foreign employment has ingrained path-dependent macroeconomic limitations on the pursuit of export-oriented trade and industrial policy (Withers 2019b). Bangladesh, Indonesia, Fiji, Pakistan, the Philippines, Sri Lanka, and Vietnam – among many others – all conform to this third category of remittance economy, though with pronounced variation in the contextually specific economic challenges and social-cultural practices surrounding migration.

Remittance economies have certain shared characteristics – namely, an economic reliance on emigration as an alternative to inclusive local development and, at the political level, an accompanying embrace of governmentality in managing and maintaining these migration regimes. However, the sheer heterogeneity of migration-development dynamics across the Asia-Pacific region precludes the possibility, or usefulness, of a singular determination of the characteristics that define an 'emigration state'. Instead, the spread of developmental challenges encountered by smaller or larger countries, with greater or lesser economic reliance on migration, implies variations in the policy objectives and apparatus of the states that govern them. This picture is further complicated by the diversity of social and cultural norms that are contested and reaffirmed amid the social transformation that occurs in the wake of widespread temporary labour migration (Castles 2010). Recognising the importance of these differences, this Element undertakes a comparative policy analysis of Myanmar, the Philippines, Sri Lanka, and Samoa to illustrate similarities and differences in how emigration policies have been designed and implemented across the region. In each of these cases, emigration policies have promoted temporary labour migration as a fix for stubborn developmental challenges while periodically reorienting to address problems arising from that very same fix. It is argued that while remittances can afford macroeconomic stability in the short run, the political backlash to the means through which they are acquired (i.e. the conditions of temporary labour migration itself) has created ongoing tensions that require active appeasement for the maintenance of state legitimacy.

The country studies included for comparative analysis were selected to represent a broad spectrum of development challenges and emigration strategies so that each offers a different angle into the political economy of temporary labour migration as it plays out across the Asia-Pacific region.

The Philippines and Sri Lanka have each been involved in widespread temporary labour migration since the 1970s, though with important differences in migration profile and the degree of state involvement in managing migration flows. Remittances are the cornerstone of the Philippines economy, accounting for 9.6 per cent of GDP in 2019 (World Bank 2023), and in many respects, it is the archetypal emigration state. The Philippines was the first labour-sending state to explicitly and actively pursue the promotion of migration as a development strategy – evidenced by extensive government investment in the training of nurses and domestic workers 'marketed' to foreign employers, as well as a subsequent rhetorical embrace of 'migrant heroism' to celebrate the economic contributions of inbound remittances (Phillips 2009; Rodriguez 2010). Low-wage temporary labour migration flows remain heavily feminised and dominated by Filipina migrant domestic workers employed in West Asia, Hong Kong and Singapore, though they are periodically interrupted by the implementation of migration bans that are used as a means of 'labour diplomacy' to address abuse and exploitation (Napier-Moore 2017; Shivakoti, Henderson, & Withers 2021). In Sri Lanka, migration has historically also been heavily feminised – with women domestic workers accounting for as much as 75 per cent of all emigration in 2005 (SLBFE 2012) – though the state has, until recently, been considerably passive in promoting and regulating emigration to West Asia. In 2013, however, following the high-profile execution of an under-aged migrant domestic worker, Rizana Nafeek, the Sri Lankan Government introduced a series of restrictions on the migration of women below a certain age or with young children (Abeyasekera & Jayasundere 2015). Nominally an effort to protect women migrant workers, the gendered migration restrictions have been widely perceived as attempting to reaffirm traditional gender norms concerning unpaid care roles (Abeyasekera & Jayasundere 2015; ILO 2018: 5–7; Weeraratne 2018a).

Myanmar and Samoa, meanwhile, are notable for their more recent temporary labour migration histories, which highlight particular challenges faced by small and fragile states. In Myanmar, undocumented cross-border migration to Thailand has been a common survival strategy since the early 1970s, as military rule established a decade earlier gradually drove the economy into a protracted decline (Khemanitthathai 2022). These workers have become an integral part of Thailand's economy and have continued to be recruited since Myanmar's military rule officially ended in 2011, but largely in the absence of any consistent migration policy framework by either government (Jirattikorn 2015). Following nascent steps towards managing these undocumented migration flows through regularisation initiatives, a subsequent military coup in 2021 has shifted emigration policies towards attempts to control emigration and remittances to stifle political opposition (Zin 2022). Like Myanmar, Samoa is one of the poorest countries in the Asia-Pacific region – classified by the UN as a 'least developed country' until 2014 (a status that Myanmar continues to hold). By contrast, though, Samoa exemplifies a 'MIRAB' economy reliant on 'Migration, Remittances, Aid and Bureaucracy' (Brown & Ahlburg 1999). Samoa has had longstanding involvement in permanent migration – largely to New Zealand, but also American Samoa and the United States (Shankman 1976; Connell 1983) – and is, after neighbouring Tonga, the second-highest remittance-receiving country in the South Pacific: personal income transfers accounted for 29 per cent of GDP in 2021 (World Bank 2023). Despite protracted exposure to labour migration as a livelihood strategy, the more recent promotion of seasonal and guestworker migration to Australia and New Zealand has given rise to concerns about the social and cultural implications of labour export – culminating in an internal review of emigration policies in 2022 (Meleisea 2023).

In surveying the migration histories and policy landscapes of these four countries, I identify three overarching expressions of governmentality within emigration policymaking – the promotion of foreign employment, the mediation of local social and economic tensions arising from migration, and the conservation of socially reproductive capacities of present and future generations – within which several more specific strategies exist. These range from the celebration of migrant workers as agents of development, to their persecution for neglecting traditional gender roles, as well as various efforts to commodify and promote 'ideal migrant subjects' in competition with other labour-sending states, implement bans to engage in labour diplomacy or mollify public concerns, and to establish transnational 'moral contracts' whereby workers pledge to uphold cultural values while abroad and states engage in jurisdictional overreach to police behaviour when they do not. These diverse permutations of emigration policymaking – as well as their implications for migrant households, relationship with domestic politics, and bearing on the so-called migration-development nexus – are the focus of this Element.

Emigration States and the Migration-Development Nexus

The relative disregard of emigration states as a subject of comparative migration analysis not only inhibits our understanding of emigration policymaking as a political process but also how these policies align with – and lend credibility to – the rhetoric of triple-win migration that has reanimated the migration-development nexus in recent decades.

The premise of triple-win migration is simple: temporary labour migration is assumed to produce mutually beneficial outcomes for labour-receiving states (who benefit from access to a flexible supply of low-wage labour), labour-sending states (who benefit from reduced unemployment and remittance inflows that provide foreign exchange earnings), and migrant households (who benefit from improved incomes and the opportunity to invest) (World Bank 2006). It is also misleading. The distribution of these 'wins' is not only unequal and reinforcing of existing regional economic disparities, but – in the case of labour-sending states and migrant households – they remain empirically unsubstantiated (Withers 2019b; Ness 2023). To date, there is no compelling evidence to suggest that remittances have a positive relationship with economic growth (Barajas *et al.* 2009; Chami *et al.* 2018). Rather, International Monetary Fund (IMF) economists have postulated the existence of a 'remittance trap' in which migrant income transfers catalyse currency appreciation (Dutch Disease) that stifles export competitiveness and reduces governmental accountability to local development needs (Chami *et al.* 2018). Meanwhile, at the household level, remittances seldom generate the investment multiplier of 'migrant entrepreneurship' anticipated by migration-development optimists (Binford 2003; Eversole & Shaw 2010). Remittances are only the residual portion of migrant workers' wages – eroded by mobility costs, associated debt, living expenses, and transfer fees – and in low-wage corridors, they often fulfil a subsistence function to provide poverty-clearing income for dependent households but not enough for significant savings or investments (Withers 2019b). Moreover, underlying structural and institutional constraints on development in migrant communities can hamper the prospect of sustainable reintegration and induce 'protracted precarity' in which migrant workers repeatedly navigate episodes of economic exclusion at home and exploitation abroad (Piper, Rosewarne, & Wither 2017). These uneven 'wins' for labour-sending states and migrant households are further compounded by broader developmental considerations, such as the education and welfare costs associated with investing in labour that is employed for the benefit of labour-receiving states (Delgado Wise 2009) and the displacement of socially reproductive labour (Burawoy 1976; Kofman & Raghuram 2015; Shutes 2021; Withers & Hill 2023).

That labour-sending states have nonetheless embraced the rhetoric of a triple-win migration-development nexus, albeit retroactively in most cases[4], is indicative of two important considerations. The first is that the developmental objectives of labour-sending states and migrant households are frequently misaligned despite having a common economic interest in obtaining remittances (albeit at different scales and for different reasons). Whereas migrant workers and their families are motivated to make lasting improvements to their social and economic

---

[4] In countries like the Philippines and Sri Lanka, widespread temporary labour migration vastly predates the post-millennial 'rediscovery' of remittances that catalysed the assumptions of 'triple-win' migration (de Haas 2012).

circumstances, these imperatives are not necessarily shared by labour-sending states preoccupied with maintaining macroeconomic stability and political legitimacy (Phillips 2009). The second related observation is that these diverging interests have occurred amid a broader political-economic transition across the Asia-Pacific, as postcolonial developmental states have progressively given way to a model of governmentality characterised by 'responsibilisation': the managed outsourcing of developmental accountability from government to governed subject (Onis & Senses 2005; Pyysiäinen, Halpin, & Guilfoyle 2017). Responsibilisation here implies a fundamental shift in the basis of governing development, not implying a 'retreat of the state' (Strange 1996), but rather a reorganisation of state functions from direct intervention to the regulation of self-governing subjects (Rose, O'Malley, & Valverde 2006). This paradigm of responsibilisation is evident throughout the domain of emigration policymaking. Longstanding developmental challenges associated with industrialisation and job creation can seemingly be bypassed via the promotion of foreign employment. In turn, workers' aggregate remittance transfers provide foreign exchange earnings that buffer against trade deficits, expand currency management options, and facilitate the repayment of external debt – providing macroeconomic stability and indirectly financing other forms of development expenditure (Withers 2019b). For emigration states, this strategy of 'migration instead of development' (Matsas 2008) offers a convenient resolution to short-term developmental problems. However, it also entrenches a deeper-seated contradiction by depending on the persistence of uneven development as a driver for continued migration and remittances, upon which macroeconomic stability now depends.

This scenario is antithetical to the objectives of the developmental state, as it has traditionally been conceived (Johnson 1982), but eminently conducive to a distinct form of emigration state that views migrant workers as 'resources that may be managed and harnessed' (Ong 2006: 6). As strategies of 'migration instead of development' become path-dependent, and remittances enshrined as a vital component of household finances and national accounting, emigration states have leveraged foreign employment as a vehicle for governmentality wherein individuals, communities, and other stakeholders assume greater governance responsibilities in lieu of the state (Chang 2018). Cast as 'agents of [their own] progress' (Rankin 2001: 19), migrant workers and their families have been celebrated as 'migrant heroes' whose personal sacrifices abroad have culminated in the remittances that help sustain local and national economies. Yet, in pursuing migration-driven development, political unrest has fomented around the exploitation and abuse of migrant workers, as well as a lack of locally available decent work and the social implications of widespread transnational family separation. Emigration states are thus caught between the need to promote continued migration for the purposes of maintaining 'migration instead of development' while also enacting policies to mitigate adverse human and developmental outcomes. The result, this Element argues, is a tendency towards policymaking that implicitly or explicitly prioritises emigration, occasionally punctuated by conspicuous interventions to address domestic political tensions, but nevertheless reinforcing an unsustainable path dependency on labour export. The short-term and inward-looking policy logic of emigration states is, moreover, identified as a significant impediment to the prospect of coordinated multilateral bargaining needed to begin rebalancing the power relations and economic outcomes of regional temporary labour migration flows.

In examining the various policy logics of emigration states, this Element offers three important contributions to the migration-development debate. Firstly, it foregrounds the persistent role of the state – recognising that 'remittance economies' cannot exist without 'emigration states' – and addresses the dearth of comparative policy analysis concerning emigration policies of labour-sending states amid academic and policymaking fixation on immigration regimes in countries of destination. This framework entails a novel conceptualisation of the emigration state itself, tracing patterns of policy convergence and divergence among labour-sending states over time to isolate defining features and contextual differences. Secondly, it offers a comparative analysis of distinctive remittance economies in the Asia-Pacific region, each representative of different migration and development policy challenges. These country studies are important because they capture both the variety and complexity of emigration policymaking across the region, as well as the centrality of these policies within contemporary development strategies. Finally, it draws greater attention to the gendered implications of emigration state policymaking – a prominent feature of which has been the implementation of bans affecting the migration of women domestic workers (Oishi 2005). The gender dynamics of migration across the Asia-Pacific region is an area of significant academic interest (Yeoh 2016), particularly regarding the social and familial outcomes of transnational separation, and the Element contributes to this still-expanding literature by bringing gender norms into conversation with emigration policymaking.

Overview of Sections

In building this argument, the Element brings together three sections of analysis that move from the general to the particular, establishing the broad political-economic commonalities of labour-sending states before interrogating with greater specificity how emigration governance has taken shape. *Section 1* elaborates on the idea of 'migration instead of development' as a framing concept for the material underpinnings of emigration states in the Asia-Pacific region, positioning earlier debates concerning industrialisation and uneven development as pivotal to the emergence of labour export strategies. It selectively reviews the literature concerning the migration-development nexus, bringing core concerns into conversation with foundational works of development economics, and outlines three central contradictions of remittance economies – the macroeconomic limitations of remittance transfers, the challenge of inclusive development, and the disruption of social reproduction – that have informed emigration policymaking. *Section 2* then links these contradictions to specific policies implemented in each of the country contexts analysed, firstly providing condensed policy histories for each country to map similarities and differences, then adopting a more Foucauldian approach to interrogate the substance of emigration governance relating to key points of tension. Finally, *Section 3* trains a more detailed focus on emigration bans and blacklists as a particularly controversial expression of emigration policymaking that situates women's bodies as sites of political contestation. It engages with what Parreñas (2021) has dubbed the 'unresolved paradox' of emigration policy – states' simultaneous promotion and constraint of women's mobility – and offers a different resolution to this quandary by foregrounding the ways in which political legitimacy has been constructed through conspicuous attempts to control women's bodies and reproductive labour. A short conclusion follows these sections, drawing together insights developed in each to argue for the significance of the observed transition from developmental to emigration states in the governance of remittance economies in the Asia-Pacific region.

1 Migration Instead of Development?

This section establishes, in general terms, the structural limitations of remittance economies throughout the Asia-Pacific region. It does so by positioning industrialisation and uneven development as centrally important processes through which to re-examine the long and contentious history of the migration-development nexus. The first section provides a selective review of the academic literature concerning the relationship between migration and development, departing from conventional analyses by foregrounding the enduring salience of foundational insights from developmental economics to contend that contemporary remittance economies are locked into a path of 'migration instead of development'. The second section then identifies three central – but frequently overlooked – contradictions of remittance economies that are considered in greater detail: the macroeconomic limitations of large remittance transfers, the perverse disincentives for promoting inclusive local development, and the implications of transnationally fragmented social reproduction. The section concludes by situating these three political and economic contradictions as informing the key domains of emigration policymaking, setting the stage for analysing country-specific policy histories and modes of governance in *Section 2*.

Revisiting the Migration-Development Nexus

International labour migration has a long and contentious association with economic development. The broad contours of the migration-development debate have been reviewed and summarised on numerous occasions (Massey *et al.* 1993; Massey 1998; Haan 2006; Faist 2008; de Haas 2010; King 2012), often in a fashion that suggests the weight of theoretical consensus has shifted back and forth over time, between positions that support or contest the assumption that international labour migration yields positive development outcomes for countries of origin (Faist & Fauser 2011; de Haas 2012). The most recent (and 'optimistic') round of the debate, and the one most relevant to the labour-sending states discussed in this Element, hinges upon the developmental potential of remittance transfers. Having eclipsed official development assistance and FDI to emerge as the largest source of foreign capital flowing into emerging economies as of 2019 (World Bank 2020), remittances serve as the fulcrum for the now ubiquitous positioning of temporary labour migration as a mutually beneficial triple-win arrangement (Wickramasekara 2011). The significance of these personal income transfers, at household and national scales, has lent new weight to claims that it is not only countries of destination that stand to benefit from globally integrated labour markets. Indeed, despite leading migration scholars' longstanding insistence that a generalisable relationship between migration and development is neither feasible nor desirable (Castles 2010), the axioms of triple-win migration have found broad support in key national, regional, and global policy fora (Piper & Grugel 2015).

In arriving at this important juncture, from which the varied logics of contemporary emigration policymaking emerge, I have no intention of again retracing the broad brushstrokes of the migration-development debate. Instead, I hope to cut a different path through the literature that places labour migration alongside the historical structures of capital formation and accumulation across the Asia-Pacific region. The rationale is to focus the lens of 'development', whose meanings are many and varied (Raghuram 2009), on what has arguably been the principal concern of postcolonial and emerging economies: agrarian transition and industrialisation. Upon independence, most former colonies inherited economies structured around the interests of European imperialism, with plantation agriculture and resource extraction predominating in their share of employment and GDP. These primary commodities provided raw input for ongoing European and North American industrialisation that, by contrast, was the engine of capital accumulation in the world economy, characterised by mass production, expanding markets, and scalable value addition that eventually yielded increasing real wages for labour. The promotion of infant industries offered emerging economies a potential route through the constraints described by the Prebisch-Singer thesis – that primary commodities experience deteriorating terms of trade relative to value-added manufactures (Ho 2008). Whether in the guise of import-substitution industrialisation (ISI) or export-oriented industrialisation (EOI), selective industrial policy was thus a cornerstone of developmental ambition for many poorer economies in the decades bookended by the emergence of the so-called 'developmental state' and its subsequent 'retreat' as consecutive Global South debt crises in the 1970s and 1980s ushered in a neoliberal turn.

For many poorer economies saddled with unmanageable public debt, strategies of state-driven industrial investment were abandoned in accordance with World Bank and IMF loan conditions requiring structural adjustment: a familiar package of governmental deregulation, market privatisation, and trade liberalisation that came to mark the Washington Consensus (Onis & Senses 2005). At the same time, emboldened by the collapse of the Soviet Union and the waning of the Non-Aligned Movement, wealthy countries continued 'kicking away the ladder' of industrial development by leveraging outsized influence in setting the agenda for international trade frameworks during enlarged negotiation rounds of the General Agreement on Tariffs and Trade and later the World Trade Organisation. In both the Uruguay and the now-stalled Doha rounds of negotiations, developed countries persistently sought to further entrench principles of free trade that impede the use of protectionist policies they implemented when industrialising (Chang 2003) and have since used regional and bilateral free trade agreements to achieve these goals in lieu of multilateral consensus. In adhering to reduced state involvement in international trade and development, few emerging economies have achieved indicators of inclusive or sustainable development (Ghosh 2019). By contrast, those economies that achieved rapid industrialisation via protectionist measures – notable examples include Japan, South Korea, and China – did experience dramatic economic growth accompanied by extensive poverty reduction, substantial real wage increases, and vastly improved human development outcomes. Indeed, any evidence to support the World Bank's claims of global reductions in poverty and inequality in recent decades invariably reflects China's remarkable industrial transition, guided by the very policies the Bank has disavowed (Hickel 2017; Ghosh 2019). In short, since the invention of the political project of 'development' in the latter half of the twentieth century (Rist 2019), the scorecard for meaningful economic transformation across the Global South can be broadly summarised as a list of those who have and have not industrialised.

Labour migration is an important part of this story, having a profound and enduring relevance to processes of industrialisation. Insofar as the economic implications of *internal* population movements are concerned, scholarly attention to this relationship predates the political project of development itself. Ravenstein's pioneering work on migration within the United Kingdom, *The Laws of Migration*, is prefaced by an understanding that 'the call for labour in our centre of industry and commerce is the prime cause of those currents of migration . . . [through which] the deficiency of hands in one part of the country is supplied from other parts where population is redundant' (1885: 198). To this end, Ravenstein takes as given that migration arises from the mutual economic interests of labour and capital, thereby coordinating the factors of production necessary to facilitate capital accumulation. Lewis's *Economic Development with Unlimited Supplies of Labour* (1954), a foundational contribution to the then-emerging field of development economics, makes this link between rural-urban migration and economic development more explicit. Taking the hypothetical example of a closed economy with a large rural-subsistence sector and a nascent urban-industrial sector, Lewis's Dual-Sector Model describes how rural-urban migration enables the absorption of surplus agricultural labour: increasing productivity, expanding capital formation in the industrial sector and – at the Lewisian turning point – increasing wages as the reserve of rural labour is exhausted (1954). The model has enduring relevance as an explanatory factor in the developmental experiences of newly industrialised economies, perhaps most obviously in China, where massive rural-urban migration has underscored the expansion of labour-intensive manufacturing along the eastern seaboard before slowing down in approach of the Lewisian turning point (Zhang, Yang, & Wang 2011; Das & N'Diaye 2013).

Yet, the 'East Asian Miracle', as it was dubbed by the World Bank (1993), is an outlier in the developmental experiences of emerging economies, the majority of which – as noted earlier – have not experienced widespread industrial transformation. As Breman's (2010) research in India suggests, internal migration does not necessarily imply the absorption of surplus labour: it can also entail the circulation of 'footloose' workers into and out of precarious employment in the urban informal sector without the capital formation described by Lewis. Historical-structural constraints and institutional barriers are major, and much deliberated, explanatory factors in accounting for stunted industrialisation across the Global South. A related consideration is the effect of international labour migration on the world economy. Indeed, a lesser discussed aspect of Lewis's Dual-Sector Model is his hypotheses relating to the effects of *international migration* in an *open-economy* setting – that is where capital, rather than ceding profits to the wage demands of a shrinking pool of local workers, seeks out new sources of surplus by 'importing' labour via immigration or by 'exporting' capital to countries 'where there is still abundant labour at a subsistence wage' (Lewis 1954: 176). These strategies are, of course, very familiar today – and find their most obvious expressions in the expansion of industrial outsourcing through FDI, on the one hand, and in the proliferation of international labour migration, on the other. In this latter scenario, Lewis determines that immigration will act as a wage suppressant within countries of destination while countervailing flows of capital to countries of origin will fail to raise real wages unless they increase local productivity (1954). In an early example of 'migration pessimism', he concludes that the free movement of labour across borders is a 'valid foundation of arguments for protectionism' (1954: 191) for developing economies.

At an abstract level of analysis, it would, therefore, seem that international labour migration has a generally inhibitive relationship with local capital formation in countries of origin. Lewis's insights, dated though they are, speak to a fundamental tension: capital will always and tirelessly seek out cheaper labour, whether by relocating productive activities abroad or by drawing on global labour reserves to cut costs at home. For countries with large labour surpluses in primary sectors of the economy, and with little extant industrial capital with which to absorb that labour, the prospect of steering industrial policy in an open-economy setting and without recourse to protectionism is highly fraught. Other demographic and geographic factors notwithstanding, it is perhaps of no surprise, then, that Asia-Pacific economies with the largest per capita international migration outflows also tend to have limited domestic industry and disproportionately high GDP shares for agriculture (Table 1). What is harder to explain, at first glance, is the historical pivot that states governing such economies have made in turning to *embrace* emigration as a fix for the stubborn challenges of development. As we shall see, the global growth of remittances and the accompanying policy agenda of triple-win migration have been instrumental in assuaging historical concerns about the migration-development nexus. In turn, an alternative paradigm of 'migration instead of development' has taken shape, wherein the structural problems associated with industrial stagnation have been superficially resolved through the macroeconomic dynamics of remittance economies.

Table 1 Net migration versus industrial/agricultural share of GDP in 2015, compared to regional and world averages (UNDESA 2016; World Bank 2024).

Country[a]	Net migration per 1000	Industry (% GDP)	Agriculture (% GDP)
Tonga	−25.4	15.5	16.9
Nepal	−15.1	13.2	26.5
Samoa	−12.8	14.5	8.3
Fiji	−12	15.2	7.9
Kiribati	−7.7	15.3	21.7
French Polynesia	−5.9	10.8	3.2
Micronesia	−5.7	6.1	26.2
Timor-Leste	−4.9	18.3	17.8
Sri Lanka	−4.7	29.5	8.2
Laos	−3.5	27.7	17.6
Tajikistan	−3.4	30.2	21.6
Kyrgyzstan	−3.3	25.1	14.1
Bangladesh	−3	26.8	14.8
Solomon Islands	−2.8	15.6	33.2
Cambodia	−2	27.7	26.6
Myanmar	−2	34.5	26.8
Turkmenistan	−1.9	54.3	9.3
Philippines	−1.7	30.5	11
East Asia		35.4	6.1
South Asia		26.4	16.7
World		26.9	4.2

[a] The table features Asia-Pacific economies with net migration rates lower than −1/1000 in 2015, the last year such data was comprehensively collected and published; war-affected countries have been excluded. There are numerous limitations in the United Nations Department of Economic and Social Affairs (UNDESA) measuring of net migration rates and these data are treated as indicative only.

Historically, international migration has been a political and economic concern for countries of origin and destination. Origin countries have been wary of a 'brain drain' as the emigration of skilled workers undermines human capital formation (Faist 2008), while destination countries have been cautious of migrant workers exerting downward pressure on the wage floor and stoking ethnic antagonism (Bonacich 1972). The global expansion of temporary labour migration regimes has ostensibly mitigated many of these concerns. Epitomised by the rigid guestworker migration schemes now prevalent across the Asia-Pacific, such regimes occupy a starring role in the rationale of 'triple-win' migration. They provide employers in countries of destination with unprecedented control over low-wage workers drawn from global labour reserves, while the very restrictions imposed on those unfree guestworkers – their short-term contracts, dependent visa status, absence of social and legal protections, lack of pathways to permanent residence and inability to be accompanied by family – enforce the *circulation* of incomes and skills back to countries of origin. Countries of destination are thus provided with an in situ spatial fix for capital accumulation and social reproduction that is at least partially insulated from domestic political repercussions due to the transience of guestworkers, their devalued location within segmented labour markets, and the welfare chauvinism accompanying visa status (Scott & Rye 2023). Countries of origin, meanwhile, are able to 'export' unemployment (and associated political unrest) in return for valuable foreign exchange earnings, thus acting as a safety valve for the fomenting pressures otherwise associated with the challenges of development (Wickramasekara 2016). The additional income earned by migrant workers, and the impact of their remittances for economically marginalised households, enshrines the presumed benefit for labour (World Bank 2006). In this formulation, temporary labour migration thus emerges as a salient remedy for the political and economic anxieties that pervaded previous eras of immigration and emigration policymaking while financially incentivising the participation of migrants and their families.

Yet, for all the rhetoric of triple-win outcomes, it is difficult to identify a single example of a migration-development 'success story'. In surveying major labour-sending states across the Asia-Pacific, whose participation in temporary labour migration has been among the longest-lasting and most voluminous globally, there is no case study where migration and remittances have been instrumental in driving local capital accumulation and GDP growth. Nor is it possible to point to an example where guestworker migration has resulted in inclusive and sustainable development outcomes for the broader economy. Far more prevalent are examples of migration-reliant economies that, through their continued integration with the lowest rungs of global labour markets, have been able to leverage aggregate remittance inflows to maintain macroeconomic stability, secure and repay international loans, and cross-subsidise import expenditure (Withers 2019b). These remittance economies lack an endogenous engine of economic growth and have become path-dependent on ever-greater migration outflows – and thus remittance inflows – to maintain a fragile and exclusionary edifice of development (Withers 2019b). At the same time, the continued supply of able-bodied workers to centres of regional and global growth effectively subsidises production and social reproduction within wealthier economies (Kofman & Raghuram 2015). The 'wins' of temporary labour migration are not evenly distributed but reinforce prevailing patterns of uneven development. In adopting a strategy of 'migration instead of development', labour-sending states have sought short-term stability at the expense of economic transformation in the long run.

The Limits and Contradictions of Remittance Economies

In considering what is potentially forgone in the pursuit of 'migration instead of development', I consider three overarching but interrelated contradictions that are common to several remittance economies of the Asia-Pacific. I firstly discuss the macroeconomic implications of large remittance transfers, which play an important role within the external sector – buffering against trade deficits, enabling greater exchange rate management options, and facilitating international borrowing – but with considerable drawbacks relating to the suppression of export industries and structural dependence on foreign labour markets. I then consider adjacent problems arising from unresolved tensions between local job creation and foreign employment, elaborating on how labour-sending states are incentivised to pursue non-inclusive growth to the detriment of achieving locally available decent work while also addressing the enduring salience of concerns relating to 'brain drain'. Lastly, I extend this analysis beyond the production boundary to consider the persistently overlooked developmental consequences of transnational family separation, addressing the commodification of care work as well as the broader implications of transnationally reorganised processes of social reproduction.

Macroeconomic Implications of Remittance Transfers

Remittances are, almost ubiquitously, positioned as the principal boon of temporary labour migration for countries of origin. This reasoning pervades multiple scales of economic life and activity (World Bank 2006). Remittances are expected to bring benefits to migrant households (which can diversify income streams, accumulate assets, and perhaps invest their earnings), local communities (which benefit from increased demand as the consumption of remittances produces multiplier effects for businesses), and the economy as a whole (as inflows of foreign-denominated currency shore up reserves and expand macroeconomic policy options). Even among more critical scholarship addressing the political economy of temporary labour migration in the Asia-Pacific region, there is typically little scrutiny of the intrinsic developmental value that remittances are assumed to carry (Skeldon 2006). Taken only as large financial injections that bolster foreign exchange earnings while apparently flowing to those most in need (Ratha 2007), there is perhaps little to quibble with. However, such an account is too simplistic, particularly if development outcomes are considered *relative* (i.e. in relation to disparities between countries of origin and destination) rather than *absolute* (i.e. in relation to improvements over historical levels of consumption in countries of origin).

To obtain a fuller consideration of the macroeconomic implications of remittance transfers in labour-sending states, we need to begin with a more fundamental classification of remittances as the *residual* wage income paid to international migrant workers. By the very fact of the capital–labour relation, we know that more value is being created by the worker than they are being compensated for, resulting in a surplus that either expands production or otherwise subsidises reproduction within countries of destination. This income is further eroded by workers' recruitment fees and travel expenses, costs of living, and remittance transfer rates so that the residual that does cross borders into countries of origin is often only a fraction of total wages earned (Kuptsch 2006; Baey & Yeoh 2015; Jones, Ksaifi, & Clark 2022). As such, any discussion of potential multiplier effects from consumption should be sensitive to the possibility that migrant wages stimulate demand in destination economies as much as or more than they do in remittance-receiving economies. This distributional consideration acknowledged, we are then tasked with tracing the 'double life' of remittances, as atomised flows of income that make their way to migrant households through formal or informal channels, but also aggregate as an influx of foreign exchange earnings held by central banks. These parallel forms that remittances assume – private income and forex reserves – are central to the overarching ways in which they are expected to yield macroeconomic benefits: directly, by increasing aggregate consumption and investment as they are spent, and indirectly, by financing imports and stabilising the local currency to facilitate international borrowing (World Bank 2006). In the context of a remittance economy where migrant workers' income transfers constitute a significant share of GDP, these two functions are mutually interrelated, though not in complementary ways.

Large and steady remittance inflows certainly drive increasing levels of consumption and investment across a given economy. However, just as an underlying lack of industrial development prevails as a structural driver of temporary labour migration, so too does it limit the extent to which this growing demand for goods and services is realised within the local economy. Though migrant households tend to spend heavily on everyday expenses, school fees, and housing – all of which are likely to produce a multiplier effect for businesses within local communities – a host of other expenses, particularly consumer durables that may be earmarked for personal enjoyment or productive ends, are likely to be import-stimulating (Phillips 2009). The long journey of a migrant worker's wage does not necessarily terminate in their home community but extends, via the purchase of consumer durables, to the capital-intensive manufacturing hubs of the global economy. For many PICs and other Small Island Developing States (SIDS), even everyday consumption may be import-stimulating, as cash-rich but time-poor migrant households are more likely to purchase imported foodstuffs than grow subsistence crops that form an important part of traditional diets (Craven 2015). Moreover, despite persistent high-level rhetoric concerning the prospects of 'migrant entrepreneurship', few migrant households invest in businesses and those that do typically involve self-employment within the informal sector (Eversole & Shaw 2010). Indicative of the persistence of developmental challenges within remittance economies, the same dearth of viable livelihoods that conditions the need to migrate for work similarly hampers the possibility of starting a business upon return.

In sum, while remittance expenditure does circulate throughout wider communities, these benefits are largely confined to the non-tradeable sector and carry little potential to change the structural composition of the economy as a whole. Rather, such expenditure tends to aggravate existing trade deficits by stimulating demand for imports, in turn creating depreciatory pressure as the local currency is sold to buy up foreign currencies in which those imports are denominated. However, the large pool of foreign exchange reserves that remittances provide is an important buffer against this tendency – allowing labour-sending states to finance imports directly or otherwise buy up the local currency, thus maintaining a relatively stable exchange rate. Plugging trade deficits and stabilising the local currency is advantageous insofar as it enables states to safeguard consumption and access international finance, but it can also produce symptoms of 'Dutch Disease', in which one sector of the economy drives currency appreciation to the detriment of export industries that are made less competitive on global markets. While this arrangement might allow a stable macroeconomic balance to be struck between imports, exports, private expenditure, and public finance, it also further ingrains a path dependency on 'migration instead of development' as opportunities to pursue EOI recede from view. This trade-off is borne out across remittance economies in the Asia-Pacific, where increasing GDP values of remittances are broadly correlated with worse trade deficits (Figure 1). This macroeconomic juggling act, in which export diversification and a structural rebalancing of terms of trade are forever deferred by the pursuit of currency stability, is the first contradiction that remittance economies grapple with.

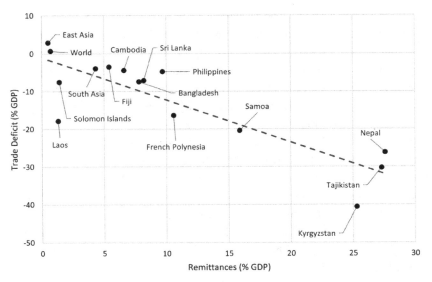

Figure 1 Remittances versus trade deficit (% of GDP) in 2015 (World Bank 2024)

Note: The figure features Asia-Pacific economies with net migration rates lower than −1/1000, excluding war-affected countries and microstates with land area of less than 1000 square kilometres. There are numerous limitations in UNDESA measuring of net migration rates and these data are treated as indicative only.

Job Creation and Inclusive Development

Amid this juggling act, the overall interests of migrant workers and labour-sending states – often taken to be aligned – diverge in important ways, leading to a second contradiction concerning local job creation. We know that, by and large, the low-wage temporary labour migration that abounds across Asia takes shape in response to a lack of locally available decent work (Yeoh 2019). Few would leave their families and work under notoriously exploitative circumstances if viable alternatives existed; most turn to guestwork to fulfil simple aspirations for a 'good life' otherwise unattainable within the confines of their local economies. Although it often takes several contracts to repay debts, purchase land, build a house, and perhaps start a business – particularly when also covering the daily expenses and school fees of dependent family members – migrant workers naturally want to achieve these goals as quickly as possible. For workers, then, temporary labour migration is foremost a sacrificial means to securing modest ends: a form of survival migration that occurs in response to uneven development and economic marginalisation within their own countries. Ideally, recourse to foreign employment would not be necessary to achieve these goals in the first instance, with local employment opportunities and other livelihoods sufficient for families to meet a poverty-clearing threshold of living.

Labour-sending states have likewise viewed the tribulations of migrant workers as a sacrifice, but with distinctly nationalistic framings that locate guestworkers as 'agents of development' – not only for their households but for the economy as a whole (Phillips 2009; Lee & Piper 2017). In the exemplary case of the Philippines, migrant workers have persistently been celebrated as 'national heroes' for indirectly facilitating development spending via the foreign exchange earnings amassed by their remittances (Guevarra 2010). As Rodriguez (2002, 2010) contends, this rhetorical valorisation has been accompanied by a new social contract, in which notions of citizenship have been transnationally extended to afford certain political rights – but also economic obligations – as a means of positioning migrant labour as an export commodity to be harnessed for development. Similar framings of migrant heroism (and obligation) have been deployed in other large remittance economies in the region, such as Indonesia (Chan 2014) and Sri Lanka (Ireland 2018), as labour-sending states have sought to leverage the needs and aspirations of migrant families to achieve macroeconomic stability. Rather than confronting the manifold challenges of local employment generation, labour-sending states actively promote and broker temporary labour migration, thereby situating unemployed and underemployed populations as an untapped resource whose labour power can be 'leased' in exchange for valuable export earnings. Here, emigration states mirror the extractive dynamics of 'immigration rentier states' recently described by Thiollet (2024). At play, however, is a fundamental contradiction in which ongoing processes of 'development' – in the form of affordable imports and remittance-facilitated loans – depend upon the continued emigration of marginalised populations to secure ever-greater remittance inflows required to sustain the model.

Under such circumstances, labour-sending states are perversely disincentivised from adopting development strategies that aspire to inclusive local development. If remittances become ingrained as the fulcrum of macroeconomic stability, and the economic marginalisation of 'surplus populations' is the key driver of emigration patterns from which those remittances are derived, then uneven development can become politically and economically durable. Labour-sending states are thus able to circumvent the onus of economic transformation traditionally ascribed to the developmental state, instead outsourcing this responsibility to their constituents, the 'working poor', for whom temporary migratory pathways are actively shaped and maintained. This diminished economic accountability is reflected by patterns of non-inclusive development spending among labour-sending states, where loans enabled by remittances have been earmarked for flagship infrastructural projects with little bearing on industrial growth or employment generation. In Sri Lanka, for example, massive fiscal commitments have been made to fund slum clearances, land reclamation, and construction projects in an effort to reimagine Colombo as a global hub for commerce and finance (Abeyasekera *et al.* 2019) – despite significant and growing disparities with rural provinces where the very basics of infrastructural development are lacking (Sakalasooriya 2021). In the Philippines, where urban-rural inequality is among the highest in Asia (Chua *et al.* 2015; Andriesse 2018), government and public–private partnership investment has likewise been concentrated on the Manila megapolis, which has been conceived as a nascent 'global city' by governing elites (Faier 2013). In both instances, remittances have indirectly financed projects that do little to arrest entrenched patterns of uneven development that frustrate poorer households' aspirations of achieving a 'good life' without recourse to exploitative foreign employment.

This second contradiction – where migrant workers' desires for locally available decent work are at odds with emigration states that find it more expedient to pursue migration instead of development – does not only manifest in divergent long-term interests of governments and their constituents. With local labour markets deprioritised in favour of foreign ones, states also relinquish considerable control over their capacity to shape human capital formation. For all the rhetoric of 'brain circulation', skills demanded by foreign labour markets rarely align with local needs, and there is ample evidence of highly qualified workers becoming deskilled by participating in temporary labour migration that, while low-waged relative to prevailing incomes in countries of destination, is nonetheless more lucrative than employment in home economies (Kofman & Raghuram 2009; International Organization for Migration (IOM) 2013). Problems, therefore, arise in training and retaining a workforce whose skills meet the needs of the local economy and can be particularly acute for SIDS, where populations are often small and fragmented, and resourcing is severely limited (Prasad 2003). If SIDS were to impose restrictions on the emigration of skilled workers, as Samoa has recently considered, this might only serve to dissuade future generations from attaining skills in the first place. At the same time, the very dependence on foreign labour markets can represent a source of vulnerability for remittance economies, as regional or global crises affecting countries of destination can affect the employment of migrant workforces and threaten the lifeline of remittance flows. When such events cause the macroeconomic balancing act to break down, as it did for Sri Lanka when foreign reserves dried up in the early months of 2022, the structural shortcomings of remittance economies are made painfully clear. Sri Lanka, which lacks developed local industry, had its currency collapse without a counterbalancing rebound in exports, prompting a general devaluation of wages and an ensuing exodus of skilled professionals seeking foreign employment by any and all means. At the time of writing, there remains a serious glut of doctors and nurses – among other professionals – that threatens the viability of the entire healthcare system (Root 2023).

Social Reproduction and Transnational Families

The third major contradiction of remittance economies is perhaps the most elementary and stems from the recognition that individual guestworker migration necessitates periods of transnational family separation that fundamentally reconfigure social reproduction within countries of origin. When workers leave their families and communities to undertake foreign employment, it is not only their *productive* labour that is displaced but also their *socially reproductive* labour – the largely unpaid work that is essential to the regeneration of biological life, the renewal of labour power, and the continuous restructuring of societal relations as a whole (Bhattacharya 2017). These latter forms of labour, principal among them the unpaid care work that sustains life daily and intergenerationally (Glenn 1992), lie beyond the so-called 'production boundary' that delimits conventional measures of the economy defined as the sum exchange value of goods and services contributing to GDP (Waring 1988). An example of Polanyi's (1977) economistic fallacy, in which the economy in general becomes conflated with its market form, the disregard of unpaid labour has been a central concern of feminist political economy. Since the early 1970s, an extensive body of scholarship has drawn attention to how unpaid care work performed within the home is a necessary function for capital accumulation (Mezzadri 2019) while also being conceived more broadly as a 'species activity that includes everything we do to maintain, continue, and repair our 'world' so that we can live in it as well as possible' (Tronto 1993: 203). For Chopra and Sweetman (2014: 409), care is moreover a social good that ' ... not only sustains and reproduces society, but underpins all developmental progress'. Yet, made 'invisible' by economic modelling, the displacement of unpaid labour – and the impairment of socially reproductive processes that depend upon it – have been chronically overlooked in the evaluation of migration-development outcomes (Withers & Hill 2023).

The most illustrative example of this contradiction emerges from the commodification of care within major corridors of guestworker migration. Driven by demographic strains and economic shifts, countries of destination have increasingly sought to position migrant labour as a fix for care provision, whether in the form of migrant domestic work in private households or the recruitment of qualified care professionals employed in institutional settings (Parreñas 2001; Yeates 2008). As with other low-wage jobs socially constructed as an extension of the domestic labour disproportionately performed by women (Elson & Pearson 1981), these avenues of care worker migration are heavily feminised. In countries like Indonesia, Sri Lanka, and the Philippines – where women have historically comprised a majority share of departures for foreign employment (Shivakoti, Henderson, & Withers 2021) – emigration states have actively promoted the 'export' of care (Rodriguez 2010). The care of hitherto unemployed women, having no counterfactual market form, is seemingly a 'free' resource to be commodified in exchange for remittances. As Truong (1996: 34) remarks, 'the tendency is to assume that women's time and labor are infinitely elastic'. Yet, with the expansion of care worker migration often outpacing commensurate shifts within gender norms that shape allocations of unpaid care work, tensions can arise around the redistribution of reproductive labour previously performed by female breadwinners. Some care practices are *aspatial* and circulate across borders with the aid of communication technologies (Baldassar, Baldock, & Wilding 2007; Ahlin 2018; Cabalquinto 2022), but many others are necessarily *proximate* and inhibited by 'immobilising regimes' that characterise guestworker migration (Merla, Kilkey, & Baldassar 2020). The prolonged absence of primary caregivers can thus result in care deficits that undermine the well-being of families and communities, bringing the economic gains of remittances into conflict with the sustainability of everyday life. As later discussed in *Section 3*, this strain has opened up a new domain of emigration state policymaking that is implicitly – and sometimes explicitly – concerned with policing the gender norms associated with work and care.

Household care practices are only one facet of social reproduction that is transnationally reconfigured during guestworker migration (Kofman & Raghuram 2015). A whole spectrum of unpaid labour is spatially and temporally displaced when women and men migrate for work, including that which supports – for example – subsistence agriculture and traditional land management practices, the building and repair of informal settlements, or participation in customary practices that maintain social hierarchies. These forms of reproductive labour relate to processes of *societal reproduction*, defined as the 'perpetuation of modes of production and the structures of class inequality inscribed within them' (Laslett & Brenner 1989: 383). While overwhelmingly conceptualised in relation to capitalist social relations, and thus sometimes inattentive to the broader array of social relations at play in Global South contexts (Mezzadri, Newman, & Stevano 2022), societal reproduction captures all the forms of labour that systematically maintain the material basis of life. Where widespread migration 'hollows out' the presence of young and able-bodied individuals who might otherwise have been involved in maintaining their communities, it simultaneously undermines the stability of social, cultural and economic structures. In small PICs that depend heavily on unpaid communal labour to maintain subsistence agriculture and mitigate against increasingly common extreme climate events, these demographic shifts can be particularly destabilising to traditional ways of life (Craven 2015). In Vanuatu, for example, recovery efforts following twin cyclones that struck Port Vila in early 2023 were reportedly hampered by a shortage of men able to repair housing in local villages. Likewise, in Tonga, migration has reduced the availability of traditional crops to such an extent that workers are required to demonstrate evidence of planting before departure; diets have nonetheless shifted towards imported foodstuffs and have been accompanied by increasing rates of obesity and diabetes, placing additional strain on already under-resourced healthcare systems (Hughes & Sodhi 2006).

A final consideration for emigration states is the fiscal expenditure associated with socially reproductive processes that occur *outside* the private activities of households and communities. If social reproduction is taken to entail the daily and intergenerational renewal of past, present, and future workers, it necessarily extends to the role of public institutions – like hospitals, schools, and welfare systems – involved in supporting workers (and non-workers) across the life course. These state functions are 'designed to secure the conditions for the profitability of capital and the reproduction of the population both as labour force and as a body of national citizens' (Jessop 2016: 143), but this arrangement is fundamentally altered in the context of significant temporary labour migration flows. With emigration states overseeing the brokerage of a significant portion of the local labour force for foreign employment, public investments in social reproduction effectively become subsidies for capital accumulation in countries of destination. For economies where temporary migrant workers constitute a significant percentage of the total workforce – as in the United Arab Emirates, Qatar, Singapore, and Hong Kong – the costs normally associated with training prospective workers or caring for retired ones are deferred to emigration states. As such, the limited returns of remittances must also be counterbalanced against the cumulative public investments made in supporting the social reproduction of workers who send them.

Emigration States and Emigration Policymaking

Together, the three broad contradictions of *remittance economies* outlined here have come to define the principal policy domains and fixations of *emigration states*. Deepening path dependencies on large remittance transfers as a source of macroeconomic stability have prompted most emigration states to adopt policies that actively promote increased temporary labour migration, whether by increasing the volume of migration within established corridors or diversifying pathways to other countries of destination, in order to secure necessary foreign exchange inflows. In doing so, emigration states inevitably have to contend with the consequences of positioning foreign employment as a substitute for local development – 'responsibilising' migrant workers as agents of national development, but also relinquishing control over the formation and retention of skills needed within the local economy, ingraining latent challenges relating to capital formation and the delivery of essential services. Finally, cutting across both issues, emigration states must contend with the thornier challenge of governing social reproduction as principal sites of social relations – families and communities – become transnationally distended, thereby fundamentally reorganising the unpaid labour practices that sustain life on a daily and intergenerational basis. Collectively, these policy domains speak to the overarching tension within the pursuit of 'migration instead of development': that the promotion of foreign employment to sustain the short-term economic stability afforded by remittances concurrently engenders a raft of longer-term and less visible social and economic insecurities that threaten the political legitimacy of emigration states. Indeed, I argue that for certain 'failed' developmental states of yesteryear – like the Philippines and Sri Lanka, for whom the ladder of industrialisation has remained out of reach – political legitimacy that was once predicated on steering local economic development has now been reconstituted upon the governance of domestic pressures stemming from mass emigration.

Yet, within this broad tension, enormous policy variation exists among emigration states. Indeed, the complexity of emigration policymaking underscores the shortcomings of existing typologies of 'labour export' (Gamlen 2019) or 'developmental migration states' (Adamson & Tsourapas 2020) that emphasise the macroeconomic mechanics of safety valve migration without attending to the contextual specificity of the limitations the strategy gives rise to. The remainder of this Element is dedicated to refining the conceptualisation of emigration states by examining how emigration policymaking has been designed and implemented with the intention of governing distinct domestic concerns that differ substantially within and between countries of origin. Partly, this recognition is grounded in the historical structures of uneven development outlined at the beginning of this section: an acknowledgement of the global geography of capital formation and the particular challenges experienced by economies peripheralised from (and by) its reach. However, it is equally a consideration of the ways in which mass emigration intersects with variegated social relations – and particularly gender norms – that occur across countries of origin, reflected in forms of state intervention that adapt to the distinctive cultural characteristics of domestic political tensions. Four country studies – Myanmar, the Philippines, Samoa, and Sri Lanka – are considered in the course of this examination. Though brevity precludes an exhaustive historical account of each emigration state, comparative analysis of emigration policymaking objectives reveals important consistencies and differences in the governance of foreign employment as a means of maintaining political legitimacy. The following section introduces these country studies and, in considering the particularities of each context, maps out key junctures at which emigration policymaking has converged and diverged in the course of recent history.

2 From Policymaking to Governance

The previous section made the case that remittance economies tend to become path-dependent on a fraught strategy of 'migration instead of development' that pits short-term macroeconomic stability against a series of longer-term obstacles to inclusive and sustainable development. Three key contradictions – relating to remittance dependency, decent work, and social reproduction – were identified as informing the key domains of emigration states' policy interventions. In this section, emigration policymaking is considered in greater detail, drawing on the contrasting approaches of four emigration states in the Asia-Pacific region – Myanmar, the Philippines, Samoa, and Sri Lanka – to reveal the complexity and contextual specificity of policy interventions. The section first offers a brief history of emigration policies in each country setting to trace the broad strokes of state involvement in regulating temporary labour migration and draw out distinctive contextual characteristics in each case. The analysis then pivots from the letter of policymaking to the spirit of governance, considering how state interventions have explicitly or implicitly responded to the contradictions outlined in the previous section and relating these to discrete facets of emigration: promotion (i.e. interventions to encourage foreign employment and increase remittances), mediation (i.e. interventions to address social and economic tensions arising from a lack of decent work), and conservation (i.e. interventions to manage the socially reproductive capacities of present and future generations). The ensuing analysis concludes that emigration states have sufficient overarching commonalities in brokering labour export to warrant typologisation but nonetheless exhibit important differences that requires a more inward-facing analysis than those offered by existing accounts.

A Potted History of Four Emigration States

In examining the scope of emigration policymaking in the Asia-Pacific region, this Element considers the policy shifts that have shaped patterns of foreign employment within four remittance economies with distinctive histories of 'migration instead of development'. The selection of these country studies for comparative analysis is purposive rather than systematic. Each country in question can be considered a remittance economy based on the volume of emigration and GDP share of personal income transfers (Table 2). However, each case likewise comprises unique characteristics that help illustrate the diversity of emigration states and the policies they adopt. The Philippines, for example, has long been considered *the* archetypal labour-export state on account of being the first in the region to comprehensively promote temporary labour migration as a development strategy; the apparatus of migration governance by and beyond the state is perhaps more developed than in any other country setting and has come to hinge upon labour diplomacy. By contrast, and despite longstanding involvement in similar foreign labour markets, Sri Lanka has taken far longer to develop the institutions and instruments of migration governance, only taking a more active stance following the end of the civil war in 2009 and doing so in a manner that has conspicuously intervened in domestic gender politics. As a small island economy with multiple colonial ties, Samoa has an extensive history of emigration. However, it has only more recently participated in guestworker schemes established by Australia and New Zealand, leveraging permissive policy environments to implement novel and frequently extra-jurisdictional forms of migration governance. Myanmar, meanwhile, exhibits a short but turbulent record of more 'mimetic' emigration policymaking where the coherence of governance frameworks has been impeded by challenges relating to the prevalence of irregular cross-border migration and the vicissitudes of domestic political turmoil.

Table 2 Migrant population and remittances in Myanmar, Samoa, Sri Lanka, and the Philippines in 2019/2020 (UNDESA 2020; World Bank 2024).

Country[a]	Total population	Migrant population	Remittances (% GDP)
Myanmar	51,483,949	3,711,751	3.4
Philippines	103,031,365	6,094,307	9.3
Samoa	203,571	135,732	17
Sri Lanka	21,336,697	1,960,025	7.6

[a] These data have known limitations and underestimate emigration from Myanmar in particular, due to the prevalence of irregular cross-border movements. They similarly do not disaggregate migrant populations according to labour market status.

The remainder of this section will elaborate on these foreshadowed distinctions by offering a condensed historical overview of temporary labour migration trends and policies in each country setting. The aim is to provide key details to contextualise the particularities of each emigration state while also drawing out similarities – junctures of policy convergence and divergence – between the four country studies. These summaries are presented in rough chronological order to facilitate a sense of historical perspective regarding the growth of temporary labour migration pathways and the corresponding emergence of emigration policymaking. Though memoranda of understanding (MOU) and bilateral labour agreements (BLAs) feature to some degree in all contexts, and the latter are prominently touted by the ILO as an avenue for strengthening protections for migrant workers, it is notable that existing research indicates that such agreements have been poorly monitored (Battistella 2012) and are largely ineffective in low-wage migration corridors characterised by weak labour market institutions and multiple avenues of labour supply (Wickramasekara 2015). Emphasis is thus placed on the underlying political-economic context of emigration governance, discussing the particularities of bilateral instruments only insofar as they are seen to have a tangible impact on the shape and outcomes of temporary labour migration flows.

The Philippines

The Philippines is often thought of as synonymous with the strategy of 'labour export' that has come to define the overarching logic of remittance economies engaged in promoting guestworker migration (Semyonov & Gorodzeisky 2004; Rosewarne 2012). This association is made for good reason. As Rodriquez (2010) details, the history of labour brokerage in the Philippines dates back to the very beginnings of US colonial occupation in 1902, when antecedent institutions of emigration took shape. The English language public education system founded by the US colonial administration, including training centres for nurses, oversaw human capital formation shaped in the image of the US labour market while nascent opportunities to migrate fostered the emergence of recruitment agents and other 'intermediaries' (Rodriguez 2010). Two waves of migration to the US – of agricultural workers during colonial occupation between the early 1900s to 1940s and of professionals (including nurses) following independence in 1946 (Gonzalez 1998) – thus established the preconditions for a third, which commenced amid political persecution and economic uncertainty following President Marcos's imposition of martial law in 1972 (Rodriguez 2010). As the Philippine Government resorted to authoritarian measures to push the economy towards a path of export-led industrialisation

(Tyner 2004), it also inadvertently pushed skilled segments of the workforce to seek foreign employment in the oil-rich economies of West Asia, where labour markets were expanding as the 1973 oil crisis dramatically increased export revenue and accelerated developmental ambitions across the Persian Gulf. Filipino men were recruited en masse for low-wage work on oil platforms and construction sites (Henderson 2021), while women increasingly found employment as live-in migrant domestic workers working for private households (Parreñas 2001). Sensing foreign employment as an opportunity to be leveraged in the pursuit of national development objectives, Marcos implemented the Philippine Labour Code in 1974 and thereby made the promotion of temporary labour migration an official government policy (Rodriguez 2010).

Emigration was thus initially seen as a means of *complementing* the industrial aspirations of a nascent developmental state – a temporary mechanism for exporting unemployment, improving the balance of payments, and augmenting national savings and investment (Tigno 2000; Henderson 2021). Though the fundamental contradictions of remittance economies outlined in *Section 1* soon foreclosed these objectives[5], the modern era of Philippine emigration nonetheless took shape as a distinctively state-driven endeavour. The Labour Code effectively nationalised the apparatus of brokerage, banning private recruitment and establishing three state agencies through which to regulate and govern emigration: the Overseas Employment Development Board (which marketed, recruited, and deployed Filipino workers), the National Seamen Board (which oversaw contracts for maritime workers), and the Bureau of Employment Services (which coordinated the national foreign employment plan and regulated private sector involvement) (Tigno 2000; Ruiz 2008). By leveraging historical institutions formed by US colonialism and deliberately integrating with emergent labour markets in the Gulf (and later Hong Kong and Singapore, among many European and North American destinations), the Philippine Government directly oversaw bourgeoning departures for foreign employment. However, as the Philippine economy became increasingly dependent on remittances to address growing external debt problems linked to excessive spending by the Marco regime (Pineda-Ofreneo 1991), emigration proved to be anything but a temporary strategy. By 1978, the scale of foreign employment eclipsed the state's capacity for labour brokerage, prompting the legalisation of private recruitment agents to help meet demand. In 1982, existing state agencies were amalgamated into a better-resourced Philippine Overseas Employment

---

[5] By the late 1970s, the Philippines's trade deficit had worsened significantly despite increasing remittance inflows, necessitating conditional loans from the IMF and World Bank that prescribed economic liberalisation measures inhibitive of the protectionist industrial policy pursued by Marcos (Henderson 2021).

Administration (POEA), together heralding the abandonment of prior industrial policy and the promotion of emigration as a permanent 'solution' for development (Asis 1992).

The POEA was mandated to implement 'a systematic program for promoting and monitoring the overseas employments of Filipino workers, taking into consideration domestic manpower requirements, and to protect their rights to fair and equitable employment practices' (Tigno 2000: 50). The emphasis placed on workers' rights stemmed from earlier government recognition that foreign employment was often highly exploitative and that, by actively promoting emigration, the state also had obligations to ensure the well-being and welfare of its citizens (Agunias & Ruiz 2007). With migration continuing apace and coming to occupy a yet more central place in Philippine social and economic life, the remit of the POEA progressively expanded to reflect the pervasive harms associated with abusive working conditions and protracted transnational family separation. Existing welfare support for workers was extended to remaining family members with the creation of the Overseas Workers Welfare Administration (OWWA) in 1987, additional labour attaches were deployed to prominent countries of destination, and the POEA began working more closely with other government departments (Tigno 2000). However, the increasing volume of migration throughout the 1980s was also accompanied by important demographic shifts. As of 1992, when the first gender disaggregated data was published, women comprised more than half of all registered departures – by 2002, this had increased to 69 per cent (POEA 2002), marking a secular trend towards feminised migration as demand for occupations in which women were over-represented, namely domestic work and nursing, outpaced recruitment for traditionally male-dominated occupations like seafaring. Migrant domestic workers, in particular, were and still are exposed to additional vulnerability during foreign employment – not only travelling to countries of destination with the tightest restrictions and fewest rights but also living and labouring in private households where there is a de facto vacuum of legal jurisdiction. Against this backdrop, rising welfare cases concerning the abuse of migrant domestic workers came to the fore of public and policy concern over emigration (Agunias & Ruiz 2007).

The 1995 execution of Flor Contemplacion catalysed a major pivot in the Philippine Government's approach to emigration policymaking. In a highly publicised trial, Contemplacion was charged and found guilty of murdering another domestic worker and a child in her care. However, this verdict was widely disputed in the Philippines, where Contemplacion's ordeal came to be seen as emblematic of the broader mistreatment of Filipino migrant workers (Romina Guevarra 2006). The execution was scheduled in the middle of national elections in the Philippines and became a flashpoint for criticism of the Philippine Government for failing to act sufficiently on the safety and treatment of migrant workers; opposition politicians, various civil society actors, and media outlets amplified the emotional outcry into a political issue, fostering a crisis of legitimacy for the incumbent Ramos government (Yeoh, Huang, & Gonzalez 1999; Alipio 2019). In response, the Philippine Government enacted two policies that have since become defining features of an emigration regime nominally predicated upon labour diplomacy (Napier-Moore 2017): (1) a retaliatory ban[6] on the emigration of migrant domestic workers to Singapore and (2) an expansion of regulatory institutions accompanied by the promulgation of policy (and rhetoric) concerning state commitments to the protection of workers. As examined in detail in *Section 3*, the Philippine Government has periodically implemented retaliatory emigration bans of this kind ever since, withholding highly demanded Filipina migrant domestic workers to negotiate improved pay and conditions through MOU (Ireland 2018). The growth of regulatory institutions, meanwhile, has deepened and broadened the state's capacity to govern migration through the auspices of protection. Critical scholarship has observed that much of this labour diplomacy comes from below (Lindio-McGovern 2013) and beyond (Rother 2022) the Philippine Government. Furthermore, there are important limits to sending-state power when it is enacted (Ireland 2018), but *being seen* to act on rights has nonetheless become a hallmark of the Philippine emigration state.

Sri Lanka

Sri Lanka's postcolonial involvement in temporary labour migration began slightly later than in the Philippines but bears some conspicuous similarities. The Bandaranaike government's attempts to implement a strategy of ISI in the early 1970s – through a 'closed economy' model that eschewed free trade to foster infant industries – ultimately worsened an already fraught balance of payment situation. Rising import costs following the 1973 oil crisis, as well as growing unemployment and the imposition of rationing measures (Kottegoda 2004), placed a significant political and economic strain on a fledgling developmental state (Kelegama 2006). Mounting pressure gave way via a dramatic regime change during the 1977 elections, in which JR Jayawardene took power on a platform of sweeping economic liberalisation (Richardson

---

[6] A similar policy had previously been implemented in 1988, to mixed success, following an abuse case in Sweden (discussed in *Chapter Three*). However, of note was the far greater volume of domestic worker migration between the Philippines and Singapore when the Contemplacion ban was enacted – Yeoh, Huang, and Gonzales (1999) report embassy estimates of as many as 80,000 domestic workers around this time.

Jr. 2004). Marking the commencement of the 'open economy' period, the Jayawardene government utilised newly created executive powers to dismantle import controls, float the currency, deregulate the banking system, and allocate export processing zones for garment manufacturing (Kelegama 2006). Emigration policies, which previously constrained foreign employment, were similarly deregulated (Gamburd 2000). The Foreign Employment Unit, created in 1976 to directly broker employment opportunities during the final embattled months of the Bandaranaike regime, was repurposed to oversee the management of newly legalised private recruitment agencies (Gamburd 2000). Temporary labour migration, almost exclusively to countries of the Persian Gulf, took off rapidly from 1977 onward – in turn prompting an expansion of consular presence in key destination countries like the UAE, Saudi Arabia, and Kuwait (Gamburd 2000). As rates of emigration continued growing into the 1980s, the government established the Sri Lanka Bureau of Foreign Employment (SLBFE) in 1985 to centralise the functions of migration governance in a similar manner to the POEA. The SLBFE was mandated to train and promote Sri Lankan workers, regulate agencies and contracts, collect data on the migrant workforce, and attend to the welfare and support of workers and their families (Gamburd 2000).

Like the Philippines, Sri Lanka's integration within Gulf labour markets was not only rapid but distinctly gendered. By the time the SLBFE was established and temporary labour migration consolidated as a development strategy, the majority of departures were of women – most employed as domestic workers in Gulf countries (Gamburd 2000). This trend is partly explained by the timing of Sri Lanka's entry into the West Asian labour market, which coincided with restrictions on the emigration of women from Bangladesh, India and Pakistan (Eelens & Speckmann 1992) – thus heightening the demand for domestic workers across the region. It was also the product of the Sri Lankan Government's eagerness to commodify the labour of women hitherto principally engaged in unpaid reproductive work within the domestic sphere of the home (Handapangoda 2024). By 1997, 'housemaids' – as the SLBFE then termed women migrant domestic workers – comprised 75 per cent of all departures (SLBFE 2022), the highest of any major country of origin at the time. However, whereas the Philippines expanded the state apparatus of migration governance in step with the deepening social and economic entanglements of labour export as a development strategy, Sri Lanka is notable for its comparatively loose regulation of migration between the 1980s and 2010s. As the civil war between the Sri Lankan Government and the Liberation Tigers of Tamil Eelam intensified, migration and remittances brought much-needed foreign reserves to assist the economic policies and military commitments of successive governments (Eelens, Mook, & Schampers 1992). Emigration itself took a relatively laissez-faire course over this period, guided by a proliferating private recruitment industry and supported by thinly staffed diplomatic missions, with greater emphasis placed on formalising remittance channels to maximise the capture of foreign exchange earnings (Rodrigo & Jayatissa 1989; Gunatilleke, Colombage, & Perera 2010).

Beginning with the 2007 creation of the Ministry for Foreign Employment Promotion and Welfare (MFEPW), government attention shifted towards the skill profile of Sri Lankan emigration, which likewise became the central concern of the 2008 National Labour Migration Policy. Skilled migration, it was concluded, would not only command higher incomes – and therefore generate greater volumes of remittances – but also resolve growing concerns about the welfare of migrant workers. In concluding that 'the ultimate protection to all migrant workers is the possession of skills' (MFEPW 2008: 10), the ministry attempted to circumvent the onus of protecting low-wage workers and their families from the adverse implications of migration while shoring up the economic returns. In practice, the latter objective entailed limited diversification of migration flows through BLAs[7] and the 're-branding' of migrant domestic workers as vocationally qualified 'housekeeping assistants' (IPS 2014). The issue of protection, though, did not go away. In 2013, Sri Lanka experienced its own Flor Contemplacion moment when Rizana Nafeek was executed in Saudi Arabia, having been charged with the death of a child in her care (Weerasooriya 2013). Nafeek, who had emigrated on falsified documents at the age of seventeen, came to symbolise the vulnerability of migrant domestic workers. Vocal protests initially demanded government action to safeguard workers' welfare but were soon adjoined by patriarchal calls to protect families from 'neglect' arising from the absence of migrant mothers. The government response, the Family Background Report (FBR), addressed both issues by implementing a partial migration ban on women domestic workers – not a bilateral *retaliatory* ban, as was the case in the Philippines, but an imposition of criteria circumscribing the emigration of women below particular ages and with dependent children (ILO 2018; Arambepola 2023). The FBR was thus not interpreted as an initiation of labour diplomacy but as a state intervention to reinscribe maternal caregiving obligations after decades of female breadwinning in the Gulf (Abeyasekera & Jayasundere 2015; Withers 2019a). The policy had an immediate impact on the gender ratio of registered departures for foreign employment, suppressing the formal emigration of women migrant domestic workers until the policy was annulled during Sri Lanka's economic crisis in 2022 (Weeraratne 2022).

---

[7] For example, with Italy and the Seychelles (Seneviratne *et al.* 2023).

Samoa

Commencing in the 1960s and accelerating in the 1970s, labour migration has been a key feature of Samoa's post-independence economy, which, like many SIDS in the South Pacific, has otherwise been constrained in its ability to follow conventional blueprints of capitalist development (Ahlburg 1991; Connell & Brown 2005). Patterns of Samoan migration reflect lines of uneven development etched by imperialism. European colonialism transformed the economic geography of the South Pacific in the nineteenth century, with the establishment of plantations in some locations mirrored by the widespread indenture of migrant workers originating from others (Graves 1986). In contrast to Kiribati, the Solomon Islands, and Vanuatu – where the colonial labour trade coercively or duplicitously recruited workers (Petrou & Connell 2023) – Samoa was designated as a location for British, German and US cotton and coconut plantations (Droessler 2018). Samoans resisted working as wage labourers, preferring to remain connected to the precolonial subsistence economy, and Samoa thus became a site of *immigration* as Melanesian and Gilbertese workers were 'brought in' to undertake agricultural labour (Droessler 2018; Petrou & Connell 2023). While not laying the foundations for the institutionalisation of labour brokerage, as had been the case in the Philippines, colonial incursions in Samoa and across the South Pacific nonetheless paved the way for future migratory pathways. A short-lived German colonial administration was succeeded in 1914 by New Zealand rule lasting until independence in 1962; nearby islands were annexed as American Samoa in 1899, which remains an unincorporated territory of the US. These past and ongoing colonial ties have been instrumental in channelling emigration flows.

For the majority of Samoa's post-independence involvement in labour export as a development strategy, emigration has been *permanent* – largely taking shape through skilled and humanitarian pathways to New Zealand, American Samoa, the United States, and to a lesser extent Australia (Connell & McCall 1990). As with the neighbouring Polynesian country of Tonga, emigration has also taken place on a massive scale, resulting in the two countries having the highest concentrations of remittances as a share of GDP in the South Pacific and, with some annual variation, globally (World Bank 2023). Connell and Brown (2005: vii) identify both countries as regional archetypes for the promotion of migration as a development strategy, noting that ' ... these two Polynesian states provide a template of remittance-dependent economy ... As long as serious economic challenges face island states, as population growth rates remain above world averages, and as expectations rise, the ability to migrate will be crucial where development prospects are few'. Their subsequent analysis shows that, across these decades of permanent resettlement abroad, Samoa had been an exception to the tendency of 'remittance decay', with strong kinship ties shaping transnational households with enduring intergenerational commitments to provide economic support to remaining family (Connell & Brown 2005). Thus, at the same time that the Philippines and Sri Lanka were constructing emigration policies and infrastructure to oversee the systematic pursuit of temporary labour migration, the Samoan Government had fewer obstacles to negotiate in securing remittance inflows.

Yet, as a SIDS where remittances have an outsized impact on all aspects of economic stability, from household to macroeconomic scales, policy involvement was eventually required to sustain 'migration instead of development'. Indeed, while Tsujita (2018) observes that the continued inflow of remittances has defied anticipation of gradual atrophy, this has involved a far more active hand from the state. Connell and Brown (2005: vii) foreshadowed that 'maintaining remittance flows at high levels therefore requires a steady flow of new migrants', and new possibilities soon emerged to secure these outcomes as New Zealand (RSE in 2007), and shortly after Australia (SWP in 2012), launched seasonal agricultural migration schemes open to workers from several PICs[8]. Samoa has been heavily involved in both schemes, as well as the later Pacific Labour Scheme (PLS), Australia's multi-year guestworker scheme that offers employment of up to four years across a broader range of low-wage industries in rural and regional locations. With numerous other remittance economies involved in these Pacific labour mobility schemes, the Samoan Government has been exceedingly proactive in securing participation. In 2014, it adopted the region's first Labour Mobility Policy, aspiring to 'promote temporary labour migration in Samoa's interests for sustainable economic growth and development' (2014: 12), and thereafter became more significantly involved in the screening and disciplining of workers actively positioned as preferable to those from other PICs. Paralleling other instances of intra-emigration state competition to provide ideal migrant subjects (Polanco 2019), the Samoan Government implemented a 'zero tolerance' policy that threatens to repatriate 'underperforming' or 'misbehaving' workers. Yet, juxtaposing efforts to increase numbers, growing reports of social issues prompted Samoa to review and temporarily suspend participation in labour mobility to consider policy options to preserve family and community life. At the time of writing, the Samoan Government remains politically indecisive about future involvement in guestworker schemes, though departures (and remittances) remain higher than many neighbouring countries.

---

[8] Participating PICs for both the RSE and SWP include Fiji, Kiribati, Nauru, Papua New Guinea, Samoa, the Solomon Islands, Tonga, Tuvalu, and Vanuatu. Australia's SWP and PLS schemes are also open to workers from Timor-Leste.

Myanmar

Regulated labour migration is a relatively new phenomenon in Myanmar, owing to two long periods of military rule between 1962 and 2011 in which international borders were, for the most part, formally closed (McGann 2013). During this period, Myanmar's national development ambitions stalled under economic mismanagement that saw the country rapidly deteriorate into the most impoverished in Southeast Asia, driving a spectrum of forced and irregular cross-border survival migration into neighbouring countries, principally Thailand (McGann 2013; Jirattikorn 2015). The Myanmar-Thailand labour migration corridor is now the largest in Southeast Asia. Involving the employment of Burmese workers in a range of low-wage industries – including fishing, food processing, construction, garment manufacturing and domestic work (Kusakabe & Pearson 2010; McGann 2013) – this corridor accounts for an estimated 70 per cent of emigration from Myanmar and approximately half of Thailand's immigration flows (Khemanitthathai 2022). The first steps towards state regulation of emigration were taken with the Law Relating to Overseas Employment in 1999, which established separate committees to formulate and implement emigration policies, and with a 2003 MOU with Thailand, which came into effect in 2009 and standardised temporary labour migration procedures in a bid to stem irregular migration (Testaverde, Moroz, & Dutta 2020). Reflective of disparities in state capacity and migration infrastructure (Jirattikorn 2015), the regularisation of Burmese labour migrants was largely driven by Thai authorities via a nationality verification process affording amnesty by conversion to legal visa status. However, the national verification process was both costly for workers and discriminatory towards Muslim Rohingya populations whose Burmese nationality was not recognised, ensuring low rates of uptake (ILO 2015). Emigration flows between the two countries remain pronouncedly irregular, as do remittances – with formal inflows constituting approximately 3 per cent of Myanmar's GDP, while informal transfers are reckoned to amount to 13 per cent of GDP (Akee & Kapur 2017).

In parallel with efforts to regularise cross-border migration to Thailand, the nascent Burmese emigration state embarked on a targeted programme of labour brokerage directed towards higher-wage labour markets in Korea, Malaysia and Singapore (Jirattikorn 2015). These formal pathways were initially male-dominated, as women were categorically not permitted to register for foreign employment until 2009, and thereafter, usually only in groups of five or more (Napier-Moore 2017). Following those reforms, domestic worker migration to Hong Kong and Singapore began taking off, with women comprising an estimated 19.5 per cent of all registered departures by 2014 (Napier-Moore 2017).

During this time, in consultation with international organisations like the IOM and the ILO, Myanmar further assembled the institutional apparatus and policy frameworks of migration governance. In 2013, a National Plan of Action for the Management of International Labour Migration was drafted with by-now familiar commitments to the 'protection and empowerment' of migrant workers and the inclusion of remittances within the national development strategy (Nogami 2017). In the same year, a National Strategic Plan for the Advancement of Women was launched, which underscored the importance of supporting the aspirations of women migrant workers (Testaverde, Moroz, & Dutta 2020). Yet, concurrent with the publishing of high-level migration frameworks (that have yet to see substantive implementation), the Burmese Government implemented a sudden series of restrictive interventions. Emigration to Malaysia was temporarily suspended in 2013 after Burmese workers were involved in violent altercations and then banned for two years in 2016 following political criticism of Myanmar's handling of the Rohingya crisis (Weijun 2018). Meanwhile, reports of mistreatment prompted bans on the emigration of women migrant domestic workers in 2014 – first to Hong Kong, then to Singapore, and later to all countries (Napier-Moore 2017). Domestic worker migration to Singapore and Malaysia resumed in 2017 and 2018, respectively, but not without having generated substantial confusion among workers, many of whom continued to migrate irregularly at far greater risk (Napier-Moore 2017; Deshingkar 2021).

The fits and starts of Myanmar's emigration policymaking suggest a notable overall lack of coherence between high-level frameworks and ad hoc state interventions. This issue echoes what Fitzgerald (2006: 283) has elsewhere observed as 'a "decoupling" of formal policy and practice that is common among weak states attempting to adopt exogenous cultural models of what modern states "are supposed to do"'. Indeed, Jirattikorn observes that 'Myanmar lacks a comprehensive and holistic migration policy or an effective migration management body' (2015: 9); rather, it appears that the state has borrowed readymade frameworks and policies that have little mutual intelligibility or efficacy in the context of the migration patterns and developmental constraints particular to Myanmar. The abruptness of policy change only worsened with the onset of the COVID-19 pandemic, which prompted further emigration restrictions and the 2021 military coup – after which the junta attempted to formalise remittance capture through state-owned banks to raise revenue and defund democracy movements (Zin 2022). As of the time of writing, passport fees have been increased to record highs, and workers are ordered to remit at least 25 per cent of their earnings via a regime-approved bank or face a three-year ban from foreign employment (San Maw Aung 2023). Against this chaotic backdrop of rapid policy oscillation and political upheaval,

Myanmar's attempts to leverage emigration in the pursuit of 'migration instead of development' appear fundamentally compromised by preceding crises of state legitimacy and the sheer prevalence of irregular migration flows resistant to hardline interventions.

Governance and Governmentality: Promotion, Mediation, and Conservation

The policy histories charted in the previous section offer some appraisal of the confluences and divergences in emigration state policymaking (Table 3). They reveal how historical structures of uneven development have been integral to the fashioning of local and international labour markets that guestworkers move between. In the cases of the Philippines and Sri Lanka especially, they also expose how the formation of emigration policies was intimately tied to frustrated attempts at industrialisation and later entailed a reorientation in the development strategies of both states. In both Sri Lanka and Myanmar, internal conflict and political unrest had an important bearing on the institutionalisation of emigration infrastructure, or lack thereof. In Samoa, the acute challenges of reckoning with the prospect of capitalist development as a SIDS have been instrumental in shaping a more recent but highly interventionist approach to regulating guestworker migration. Similarly, belated but assertive emigration policymaking was seen in Myanmar, but longstanding irregular migration flows and enduring political turmoil have exacerbated an apparent lack of efficacy in the rapid appropriation of frameworks and strategies that have been put to use in other emigration state contexts. Collectively, there is a common ambition to situate temporary labour migration as a substitute for inclusive local development that can also be observed (with similar inconsistencies and idiosyncrasies) in other emigration states across the Asia-Pacific region – including Bangladesh (Rahman 2012; Deshingkar *et al.* 2018; Wu & Kilby 2023), India (Irudaya Rajan & Joseph 2015; Joseph *et al.* 2022), Indonesia (Silvey 2004; Rosewarne 2012), Pakistan (ILO 2020), and swathes of the South Pacific now heavily integrated in regional labour markets (Petrou & Connell 2023).

What these policy histories do not adequately convey, though, are the larger objectives and techniques of migration governance itself. A growing body of scholarship has fruitfully drawn on Foucauldian notions of *governmentality* – that is, 'the reciprocal constitution of power techniques and forms of knowledge' (Lemke 2001: 191) – to examine how immigration and emigration policies intervene to manage the habits and behaviour of self-governing migrant subjects (Raghuram 2009; Gamlen 2014; Hoang 2017; Chang 2018; Parreñas 2021; Gunaratne 2023; Thiollet 2024). This self-governance, the inculcated

Table 3 Summary of selected emigration policies.

Emigration Policy	Myanmar	The Philippines	Samoa	Sri Lanka
Dedicated Governing Body for Emigration	No – falls under the remit of the *Ministry of Labour, Immigration, and Population*	Yes – POEA (1982–2021), superseded by DMW (2021–present)	No – falls under the remit of the *Ministry of Commerce, Industry and Labour*	Yes – SLBFE (1985–present)
State-Facilitated Recruitment	Yes – limited to particular schemes, like Korea's EPS; recruitment agencies are highly restricted	Yes – directly and via the regulation of licenced agencies	Yes – directly and via the regulation of licenced agencies	Yes – directly and via the regulation of licenced agencies
Pre-departure Training	Yes – mandatory for foreign employment, except emigration to Thailand	Yes – mandatory one-day sessions for all workers and additional three-day sessions for migrant domestic workers	Yes – mandatory one-day pre-departure briefings	Yes – mandatory twenty-one-day certified training course for women migrant domestic workers
Labour Attache	Yes – in Thailand and Malaysia	Yes – including Hong Kong, Singapore, Malaysia, Japan, Korea, Taiwan, Saudi Arabia, UAE, Bahrain, Kuwait, Lebanon, and Qatar	Yes – in Australia and New Zealand	No – welfare support from diplomatic missions only

Welfare Support for Migrant Households	No	Yes – social assistance and insurance schemes implemented by OWWA	No	Yes – limited social insurance schemes implemented by SLBFE
Reintegration Programmes	No	Yes – financial literacy and business training run by the National Reintegration Center	No	Yes – support for self-employment scheme run by SLBFE
Migration Bans	Yes – total ban to Malaysia in 2013; conditional bans to multiple countries in 2014	Yes – multiple country-specific bans between 1988 and 2018	No	Yes – conditional ban to multiple countries via FBR (2013–2022)
Blacklisting	Yes – targeting the remittance patterns of individual workers	No	Yes – targeting the personal conduct of individual workers	No
Relevant MOUs and BLAS	MOU with Thailand (2009)	BLA with Qatar (1997); MOU with Bahrain (2007), Japan (2009), Jordan (2010), Korea (2009), Kuwait (1997), Lebanon (2012), Taiwan (2003), UAE (2007)	MOU with Australia (2018) and New Zealand (2014)	BLAS with Israel (2020), Saudi Arabia (2014) and Qatar (2008); MOU with Bahrain (2008), Korea (2004), UAE (2018), Jordan (2012)

'conduct of conduct' (Rose, O'Malley, & Valverde 2006: 101) implicit in the divestment of state functions to responsibilised actors, is the very stuff of governmentality – and what sets it apart from more conventional analyses of governance. Consequently, the management of migration cannot be the exclusive domain of reified nation-states. It is a more diffusive exercise of power, driven by dominant ideologies and mutually co-constituted by a constellation of actors spanning migrant workers, recruitment agents, local and transnational civil society organisations, and international organisations. Within this busy picture, the state has occasionally gone missing (LeBaron & Phillips 2019). Sandwiched between expanding global governance from above and a variety of ever more globally interconnected networks from below, the enduring role of the state is often understated by transnationally attentive scholarship, not least because many of its core functions have been 'outsourced' to these non-state actors. Yet, this does not itself suggest a withdrawal of the state. Governmentality is helpful in accounting for instances where fewer *direct* state interventions might nonetheless be accompanied by greater *indirect* responsibilisation of individuals and intermediary organisations, thereby reducing state accountability while retaining regulatory control over the social and economic tensions bound up in migration (Joseph *et al.* 2022). The apparent 'retreat' of developmental states has, to varying degrees, been accompanied by the 'advance' of emigration states that situate migrants as 'resources that may be managed and harnessed' (Ong 2006: 6), representing not 'less government' but 'new modalities of governance' (Ferguson & Gupta 2002: 989).

In light of these considerations, and notwithstanding the importance of those actors operating beyond the ill-defined boundaries of the state, the remainder of this section hones attention on emigration states' involvement in migration governance. It returns to the three central contradictions of remittance economies outlined in *Section 1* – remittance dependency, decent work, and social reproduction – and considers how emigration state policymaking has interfaced with governmentality in response to these tensions. In doing so, each of these principal social and economic contradictions is related to a different aspect of emigration policymaking in which the relevance of the fundamental problem they contain is most pronounced: promotion, mediation, and conservation.

Promotion

The promotion of temporary labour migration is a ubiquitous feature of emigration states and, with securing greater volumes of income transfers a central objective, is reflected by various efforts to increase departures, improve prevailing wages, or enhance remittance rates. As Polanco (2019) argues, these strategies frequently take place in a context of competition among emigration states looking to export labour to a limited number of foreign labour markets to which they have ready access. Thus, beyond general approaches to maximise remittances – such as deregulating recruitment and encouraging feminised migration on the assumption that women will remit more (Oishi 2005; Rosewarne 2012) – emigration states have engaged in 'competitive differentiation' by managing the 'branding' (Guevarra 2014; Polanco 2019) and 'marketing' (Parreñas 2021) of their workers. Most widely documented in the case of the Philippines, where the state runs pre-departure orientations to *discipline and socialise participants into being energetic, 'superior' workers* (Polanco 2016: 1337), similar strategies can be observed in the Sri Lankan Government's explicit articulation of the need to 'rebrand' domestic workers as certified 'domestic housekeeping assistants' to command greater wages within Gulf labour markets (IPS 2014). In Samoa, which is in direct competition with nine other countries to supply labour through relatively small guestworker schemes in Australia and New Zealand, the promotion has gone further still. In response to employer concerns about the physical and mental perseverance of seasonal agricultural workers, the Samoan Government introduced intensive physical fitness screening (Likou 2017), pre-departure briefings in which workers and families sign moral contracts pledging to uphold Samoan values (Lafoai 2021), and a 'zero tolerance policy' through which chiefly power structures are leveraged by threatening to blacklist the participation of entire villages if one of their workers is reported for 'performance' or 'disciplinary' problems (Samoa 2017). Emigration states thus intervene to co-produce with immigration states what Hahamovitch (2003) describes as 'perfect immigrants' who are readily disciplined, easily deportable, and self-reliant in adversity.

The concurrent interplay of emigration state promotion strategies and longer colonial histories of uneven human capital formation has come to mark foreign labour markets as segmented by racialised hierarchies of migrant labour (Rosewarne 2012; Nishitani, Boese, & Lee 2023). Yet, as emigration states jostle to discipline and promote reputable guestworkers, so too do they require migrants to internalise and self-regulate these characteristics. Here, governance frameworks become more diffusive, relying less on the direct training and conditioning of workers and more on the cultivation of acquiescent ideologies through responsibilisation. In Samoa and other SIDS, where the supply of prospective workers far outstrips foreign demand for their labour, this is readily achieved through employer monopsony itself. Employers are routinely invited to screen and interview large pools of prospective workers, who compete to best exhibit the desired attitudes, work ethics, social qualities, and cultural acumen that pre-departure briefings emphasise. Workers I have interviewed in Australia have consistently expressed their gratitude for the opportunity of foreign employment, despite admissions of unfair treatment, and all espoused some variant of the intention to 'work hard, not cause trouble, and send money home'. They are likewise reminded, via outlets ranging from social media groups to ministerial addresses, that they are 'ambassadors' of Samoa whose performance abroad carries implications for the nation's collective well-being. The cultivation of these sentiments, of course, has antecedents in the state-promulgated rhetoric of 'migrant heroes' in the Philippines and Sri Lanka. However, in those contexts, where wage differentials are slimmer[9] and foreign employment is arguably more exploitative, a more direct involvement of the state can be observed in the celebration of workers' contributions to national development (Ireland 2018). Indeed, the framing of migrant workers as 'agents of development' has been altogether more pervasive in those contexts, where a greater need to reinforce the credence of temporary labour migration is underscored by those states' abdication of alternative projects of industrial development.

Mediation

Emigration states are also active in governing the mediation of social and economic tensions relating to temporary labour migration and the availability of decent work, most notably with regard to the protection of workers' rights and conditions abroad. Nonetheless, 'protection' has been approached very differently from one country setting to another. Though sharing 'an equally intense and consistent impetus to control female domestic workers' migration' (Ireland 2018: 325), a distinctive rift exists between the lack of support extended by the Sri Lankan Government and the comparatively robust and interventionist approach adopted by the Philippines (Gamburd 2009). The Government of Sri Lanka has primarily addressed protection through an ethos of paternalism, using pre-departure training to inculcate docility and compliance to ostensibly minimise the likelihood of altercations (Handapangoda 2024), and through enforcing age-based emigration restrictions that similarly imply an individual responsibility for safety (Arambepola 2023). Though private recruitment agencies and unlicensed subagents are known to be complicit in undermining workers' rights and conditions (MFEPW 2008), the government has only made superficial gestures towards long-promised regulatory intervention (Weeraratne 2018b). Its approach instead resembles what Chang identifies in Indonesia as a 'liberal rationality of protection' that positions vulnerable migrants as 'self-regulating subjects' (Chang 2018: 695). By

---

[9] Within Australia's PALM scheme, workers can reportedly earn up to 10 times local hourly rates (Doan, Dornan, & Edwards 2023).

contrast, the Government of the Philippines has been far more assertive in advocating for its foreign workers, using a well-developed diplomatic apparatus to engage on rights issues with notoriously obstinate receiving states in the Gulf and Southeast Asia, particularly in the years following Contemplacion's death. This not only reflects the politics of an emergent transnational social contract, wherein the developmental obligations of workers are matched with state protections (Rodriguez 2002), but heightened bargaining power owing to Filipina migrant domestic workers coveted status in foreign labour markets. By withholding the supply of migrant domestic workers to particular countries, the Government of the Philippines has occasionally been able to negotiate improved conditions that benefit workers and the remittance economy. As Ireland (2018) has argued, this strategic contingency actually enables the Philippines to strengthen the 'branding' of its foreign workforce.

By contrast, Myanmar's more incongruous adoption of ambitious rights-based frameworks and kneejerk use of country-specific bans in the name of protection is perhaps best understood as an example of what Gamlen (2014: 202) terms *mimesis* – that is the modelling of policies based on perceived similarity. The ineffectiveness of these policy interventions reflects compromised state capacity and the long-documented inability of any state to meaningfully 'control' formal migration flows where irregular alternatives exist. In other words, Myanmar exhibits a lack of governance in the mediation of migration issues and is instead notable for implementing policies shaped by the constitutive power of international organisations (like the IOM and ILO) and other state actors (like the Philippines) that have little bearing on its own capacities and circumstances. Samoa, meanwhile, offers a remarkable counterexample – actively extending its own legal and institutional frameworks across national jurisdictional boundaries. In 2019, Samoa became one of the first countries in the South Pacific to employ a 'country liaison officer' as an official overseas point of contact for workers concerned about welfare and working conditions in Australia and New Zealand. Though their official role is to support and protect the rights of Samoan workers, liaison officers have been referred to as the 'eyes and ears' of government, responsible for ensuring 'that they [workers] do not break any laws or cause trouble, which may undermine government efforts to secure more jobs for Samoans' (Samoa Global News 2019). Video footage has since emerged of a liaison officer demanding that workers in Australia leave their labour union, informing them that the Samoan Government 'doesn't allow you to join the union' (Schneiders 2022), while several other workers have reported that their complaints of mistreatment were ignored (Keresoma 2022). Mediation, in Samoa's case, is largely a matter of disciplining workers in a manner consistent with strategies of promotion.

Importantly, mediation not only relates to the governance of social and economic tensions that migrant workers might encounter while they are abroad but also those they navigate when they return home. The proliferation of 'triple-win' migration rhetoric has been accompanied by the incessant framing of migrants and their families as entrepreneurial subjects whose remittances are expected to 'empower' them to consume and invest their way out of poverty – an obligation once designated as the responsibility of the developmental state (Teo 2024). Implicit in this responsibilisation is a reduced role for the public provisioning of emigration states, as migrant households' expenditures on private schooling fees and healthcare costs come to be seen as synonymous with positive human development impact, and job creation itself eventually becomes the preserve of migrant entrepreneurs. Emigration states' complicity in these forms of governmentality is most apparent in longer-established remittance economies, like the Philippines and Sri Lanka, where the contradictions of non-inclusive growth have played out over decades[10]. In the Philippines, state agencies such as the OWWA and the National Reintegration Center augment expectations of migrant entrepreneurship by providing financial literacy training, business development workshops, and enterprise loans in keeping with the objective of encouraging returned workers to 'work and live with [an] entrepreneurial mindset' (IOM 2023). Fewer sources of institutional support exist in Sri Lanka, though the SLBFE now runs a 'Support for Self-Employment' programme that offers loans for recently returned migrants (SLBFE 2023). In both cases, government failure to create locally available decent work as an alternative to survival migration has been obfuscated by the rhetorical celebration of migrant workers as heroic agents of development whose aspirations for a better life are politically manoeuvred towards the promise of entrepreneurial success.

Conservation

Finally, emigration governance has intervened in the conservation of social life when guestworker migration and transnational family separation threaten the sustainability of processes and institutions that knit the social fabric. Particularly in the context of feminised emigration, though not exclusively, states have sought to redress the displacement of socially reproductive labour that it has actively commodified as a labour export, as well as adverse social outcomes for children of migrant households. At the most benign end of the

---

[10] Though remittance-led enterprise has so far been absent from Myanmar's stalled embrace of emigration governance, supporting returned migrants' business investments was a key theme of the 2023 Pacific Labour Mobility Annual Meeting (a multistakeholder forum that coordinates regional policymaking priorities for the PALM and RSE schemes that Samoa participates in).

spectrum, these strategies have included the extension of welfare support to migrant households requiring additional resources and the creation of reintegration frameworks intended to support the return of foreign workers. However, where these frameworks have been developed, as in the Philippines, they are often piecemeal and dependent on the involvement of an array of civil society organisations that step in to provide informal social assistance (Henderson 2021). More extreme interventions can be observed in Sri Lanka and Samoa. In Sri Lanka's case, the FBR that was introduced after Nafeek's death in 2013 introduced a raft of restrictions on the emigration of women with young children intended to reinforce culturally ascribed gender norms relating to caregiving. Whereas studies in other remittance economies have shown a considerable degree of flexibility in gender norms during migration (Yeoh 2016), decades of female breadwinner migration from Sri Lanka has been accompanied by persistent gender disparities in the performance of unpaid care work (Jayaweera & Dias 2009). The FBR thus responded to an emerging moral panic that, as Sri Lanka became 'a country of housemaids' (Yahampath 2013), the institution of the family would itself fall apart. In Samoa, similar concerns have arisen around the prevalence of extramarital affairs and the social implications of relationship breakdowns, resulting in further extra-jurisdictional government interventions where workers found 'guilty' of adultery can be 'stood down' (i.e. have their employment terminated) and blacklisted from future participation in guest-worker schemes (Government of Samoa 2017).

Interestingly, the Government of Samoa has been more vocal than other emigration states in articulating concerns about the broader gamut of socially reproductive processes and institutions affected by migration – including the sustainability of village life, impacts on the church, and the shaping of future workforces. In 2021, the Prime Minister announced that changes to existing promotion strategies were needed to preserve Samoan communities and their way of life (Samoa Global News 2021), eventually responding to growing political pressure to act by pausing Samoa's participation in Pacific labour mobility schemes to Australia and New Zealand while the government conducted a review of both programmes (Government of Samoa 2022). Following the review, a newly published Samoa National Employment Policy nonetheless reaffirmed the need to expand overall participation, with the caveats that the government would target a wider array of industries and continue to 'manage the attitudes of labour mobility workers and impose sanctions on them if needed' (Government of Samoa 2022). Upon the resumption of emigration, further assurances were given that a new Labour Mobility Policy would ensure 'strict observation of social, cultural, and moral values' (Feagaimaali'i & Fotheringham 2023). Since then, the Samoan Government appears caught between the short-term impetus to increase remittances and the longer-term implications for the Samoan economy, with Prime Minister Fiame Naomi Mata'afa stating that Pacific nations are 'not merely outposts to grow labour' for developed nations and reaffirming that the 'brain drain' remains a pressing issue (Dziedzic, Voloder, & Raela 2023). These concerns find a cautionary tale in the recent experiences of Sri Lanka, whose fragile and debt-laden remittance economy imploded in 2022, resulting in the unprecedented exodus of skilled professionals whose incomes collapsed alongside the rupee. Now facing critical labour shortages across multiple industries and essential services, the incumbent Prime Minister Ranil Wickremesinghe has called for industrialised countries to pay reparations in compensation for the brain drain experienced across the Global South (Abeysinghe 2023).

The Tensions of Emigration Governance

This section has shown that, in the pursuit of labour export as a substitute for local development, emigration states have some important shared characteristics. They broker labour exports, develop accompanying regulatory frameworks and institutions, and periodically intervene during crises. However, it has also demonstrated crucial differences in the way emigration states have designed and implemented policies over time, as well as the link between policymaking and the broader imperatives of governance as states varyingly outsource the onus of development to responsibilised subjects that drive the remittance economy. In taking this Foucauldian turn, it has exposed multiple and occasionally inconsistent techniques of governmentality at play from one country setting to another, at once reflecting the particular circumstances and characteristics of those remittance economies but also a discernible strain between competing economic and political logics more generally. These tensions run through key facets of emigration policymaking, through which states promote emigration by attempting to cultivate ideal migrant subjects to be exploited in foreign labour markets while also seeking to mediate the welfare of those workers without undercutting remittance flows and conserve socially reproductive capacities across a variety of processes and institutions that have been transnationally reconfigured. One key observation that emerges from the complexity of emigration governance, though, is the political importance of these interventions. Just as de Haas (2023: 303) has recently concluded of immigration regimes across the Global North, where 'bold acts of political showmanship conceal the true nature of immigration policies', so too do emigration states seek political returns on the concealment or superficial redress of problems associated with 'migration instead of development'.

The migration bans and blacklisting strategies alluded to throughout this section are the most emblematic examples of this double logic enacted by emigration states and are set aside as the subject of greater consideration in the following section. Here, the gender politics that have thus far been implicit in the three central contradictions of remittance economies are more explicitly analysed. The promotion and restriction of women migrant workers lies at the very heart of the tension between the pursuit of remittances, the protection of 'vulnerable' workers, and the sustainability of socially reproductive processes.

3 Of Bans and Blacklists

This final section adopts an explicitly gendered lens in focussing upon one of the most prevalent and controversial forms of emigration state policymaking: emigration bans. Bans have a long and turbulent history in the Asia-Pacific region. They have become increasingly common as emigration states seek to reconcile the stubborn tensions inherent to remittance economies by promoting emigration for economic gains and constraining the mobility of *some* to achieve political objectives. In some contexts, bans have been used as a method of initiating labour diplomacy. In others, they have been used as a means of reinforcing gender norms and traditional values as migration begets politically contested forms of social transformation. In both scenarios, female bodies are overwhelmingly the site of intervention[11] and control over the productive and reproductive labour of working-class women the primary policy fixation. In exploring examples from each of the four country settings outlined in the previous section, it is argued that the seemingly paradoxical promotion and constraint of migration cannot be explained by welfare concerns alone but rather reflects contextually specific ways in which political legitimacy has been constructed with reference to gender norms and the selective control of women's bodies through 'gendered border regimes' (Hwang 2018). The section concludes by suggesting that, in all cases, emigration bans have lacked efficacy in altering the practical outcomes of temporary labour migration – but that iterative and increasing usage by emigration states reflects enduring political value as conspicuous displays of state power.

The Unresolved Paradox of Emigration Bans

Parreñas (2021: 1044) introduces the 'simultaneous promotion and protection of domestic worker migration in sending-state migration governance' as an 'unresolved paradox' of emigration policymaking. On the one hand, certain

---

[11] Though not exclusively, noting that men also perform migrant domestic work, and that male bodies are also the subject of emigration policymaking – as the case of Samoa demonstrates.

perspectives have observed emigration states as willing to suspend the economic gains of foreign employment to stage 'value-laden' interventions to defend the well-being of migrant workers (Oishi 2005). On the other, emigration states have been charged with leveraging labour export as an unabashedly extractive process that produces harm in the pursuit of remittance inflows (Rodriguez 2010). Parreñas's formulation of these apparently contradictory governing logics fore-grounds one of the overarching tensions identified in the previous section: that by promoting the emigration of workers disciplined into subservience, emigra-tion states market their foreign workforces as compliant and exploitable, thereby engineering situations of vulnerability that require redressing lest cumulative instances of abuse manifest as political dissent (Parreñas 2021, 1059). Parreñas convincingly resolves this paradox in the case of domestic worker migration in the Philippines, drawing on the overlooked importance of 'pastoral power' to argue that the overall continuation of the labour-export model has required the state to both ensure migrant domestic workers' acquiescence to the authority of foreign employers (to sustain demand) and cultivate resistance to the abuse of that authority (to sustain support). Thus, workers are disciplined as 'self-regulating subjects' but also 'self-advocating subjects' (Parreñas 2021: 1051). However, the conclusion that emigration states equally 'promote migration and protect migrant workers' (Parreñas 2021: 1060) is an extrapolation from the Philippine context, the generalisability of which is troubled by countervailing examples where emigration states impose migratory restrictions with little bearing on the well-being of workers.

Considering 'migration bans' from a wider perspective that includes prac-tices of 'blacklisting' prevalent throughout the South Pacific, this section considers how restrictions on emigration have been implemented in the Philippines, Sri Lanka, Myanmar, and Samoa. Comparative analysis confirms key aspects of Parreñas's (2021) thesis: that emigration states engage in seem-ingly contradictory efforts to promote and constrain foreign employment, that these disciplinary interventions are laced with gendered subjectivities, and that states' attempted reconciliation of economic and political priorities is the underlying explanatory factor. It also makes important departures, namely by revealing how protection in the form of labour diplomacy has a particular political purchase in the Philippines that is by no means shared in other emigration contexts. Rather, reflecting Fraser's (1997) useful distinction between 'affirmative' and 'transformative' remedies to injustice, wherein the former category involves superficial forms of redress that leave the structural causes of a given problem unstirred, migration bans and blacklists are situated as complex and 'inward facing' techniques of governmentality that can garner political legitimacy without actually protecting workers' well-being. Moreover, it will be shown that such bans are often unaccompanied by a genuine economic trade-off, instead driving migrant workers into risk-laden irregular migration that heightens the conditions of vulnerability. The section begins by examining the case of the Philippines, from which Parreñas's (2021) conclusions are derived. It then offers a stark contrast in the case of Sri Lanka, where emigration bans have been mired in a politicisation of women's bodies and reproductive labour, and in Myanmar, where bans have had little bearing on migratory realities. Finally, it considers a fundamentally different approach to bans in the form of Samoa's policy of blacklisting workers, which, while not directed towards women migrant domestic workers, is nonetheless seen as an attempt to 'protect' women by reaffirming the gendered institutions of social reproduction.

The Philippines

The Philippine Government sends mixed messages to women by encouraging their participation in paid work outside of the home, institutionalised through the training and promotion of domestic workers (Rodriguez 2010), without contesting norms that situate their 'proper place' as being inside the home (Parreñas 2008). This is a contradiction that, in some respects, is inherent to the commodification of care work – which simultaneously assigns an *exchange value* to care (i.e. as a labour export) while neglecting the *use value* of that same labour in the local economy (i.e. as unpaid work essentialised as feminine). However, unlike in Sri Lanka, where the gradual exposure of this contradiction has been accompanied by fomenting political pressure to reconstitute gender norms around a patriarchal model of male breadwinner and female caregiver, public anxiety over women's work and care roles have seemingly been less instrumental in prompting migration bans in the Philippines[12]. Indeed, migration has come to be associated with good mothering insofar as it enables women to provide for their children (Parreñas 2005). Public concern has instead taken shape around a different contradiction, one where the government openly celebrates the sacrifices of millions of 'migrant heroines' but takes little action to prevent instances of abuse or responsibility in providing alternative local employment. As Guevarra (2006) has argued, Flor Contemplacion thus became publicly construed as a martyr who symbolised the economic plight of poor Filipina women pursuing migration as a pathway out of poverty, partly in response to the failure of government to

---

[12] An important exception exists with regard to the moral panic surrounding irregular sex worker migration, whereby the government of the Philippines has exercised disproportionate and discriminatory restrictions on the mobility of working-class women emigrating on tourist visas (Hwang 2018: 516).

create viable livelihoods at home. Action was demanded, not to curtail the transnational livelihoods of migrant women, but to deliver justice by extending 'protection' – both by halting migration to offending states in the short-term and through negotiating better conditions going forward (Ireland 2018). Thus, while the Philippines was not the first emigration state to enact gender-based migration restrictions (Eelens & Speckmann 1992; Shah 2013), it is notable for implementing bans as a policy for intervening in the protection of workers labouring in long-established and economically lucrative migration corridors.

The Philippine Government has adopted a tendency to exercise country-specific bans in response to crisis events, beginning with a total migration ban imposed in 1988 following the abuse of a domestic worker in Sweden and followed by the 1995 country-specific ban on migration to Singapore in the aftermath of Contemplacion's execution, as discussed in *Section 2*. Subsequent bans have been placed on domestic worker migration to Lebanon in 2006, as well as to Jordan in 2008, to Saudi Arabia in 2011, and to Kuwait in 2018 (Henderson 2021). In these cases, the Philippine Government has attempted to use bans as a means of addressing two objectives: quelling politically sensitive public outrage swelling in the aftermath of abuse scandals and, secondarily, applying pressure on banned countries of destination to commit to improved working conditions for domestic workers (Henderson 2021). Domestic worker migration bans thus offer a means of being seen to 'act' and thus recover political legitimacy in the face of widespread scrutiny. At the same time, by enacting country-specific bans, the economic rationale of temporary labour migration is also safeguarded – women migrant domestic workers remain free to travel to other destinations, ensuring a continuation of remittance flows, while pressure can be applied to specific 'bad actors' to improve standards and protections as a condition for resumed migration. The 2018 ban on domestic worker migration to Kuwait is a key example of this tactic; the ban was lifted within a year in return for the Kuwaiti Government signing a new MOU guaranteeing workers greater rights and protections (Henderson 2021). This exercise of pastoral power, itself enabled by the racialisation of state-disciplined Filipina migrant domestic workers in heavily segmented foreign labour markets (Ireland 2018), has become an integral basis for preserving state legitimacy in the context of a remittance economy that systematically produces harm. Indeed, despite setting internal targets for registered departures and remittance inflows, the Philippine Government claims to no longer *promote* migration but only *protect* workers (Parreñas 2021).

Sri Lanka

Though the disciplining of women's bodies and emotions has consistently been a fixation of efforts to promote migration (Handapangoda 2024), the Government of Sri Lanka has only recently embraced a domestic worker migration ban as a component of emigration policymaking. Like the Philippines, a crisis event catalysed policy change, with Nafeek's 2013 execution provoking political outrage over the abuses endured by migrant domestic workers in the Gulf. However, in the media coverage that followed, articulations of collective moral harm relating to the abuse of women migrant workers became interwoven with distinctly patriarchal unease about the presumed neglect of families 'left behind' by migrant mothers (Withers 2019a). The steady feminisation of migration had long been accompanied by moral panic about women abdicating from domestic obligations (that men could or would not perform), and Nafeek's death provided a pretext to politicise these concerns. The Sri Lankan Government responded with the implementation of the FBR, discussed in *Section 2*, which introduced age-based restrictions on the emigration of women to particular countries (a response to Nafeek's underage status when brokered to Saudi Arabia). It also introduced a series of restrictions on women's migration where it would compromise expectations of maternal caregiving (Abeyasekera & Jayasundere 2015). Women with children under five were outright prohibited from migrating, while women with children older than five were required to complete an FBR report – involving the identification of a 'suitable' female guardian for dependent children and attaining spousal consent – subject to government inspections and approval (ILO 2018). In contrast to bans periodically implemented by the Philippine Government, pressure was not exerted on specific countries of destination to improve working conditions but on the overt defeminisation of migration itself – linking the exploitation and abuse of women migrant domestic workers to currents of paternalistic politics, already present in government publications (Rajapaksa 2005), calling for women's contribution to 'the nation' to be *rearticulated* through the site of the home and care for the family (de Alwis 1996).

While consistent with responsibilising women domestic workers as 'self-regulating subjects', the FBR marked a jarring policy break with the government's longstanding strategy of promoting domestic worker migration as a developmental strategy. A lack of explicit attempts to direct the FBR towards bilateral labour negotiations that might improve the rights and conditions for women migrant domestic workers in countries of destination lends weight to analyses that situate motivations for the policy shift in local political concerns (Abeyasekera & Jayasundere 2015; Withers 2019a; Gunaratne 2023). While domestic worker migration has been a major export earner for Sri Lanka, it has also – over decades – been instrumental in challenging patriarchal norms that have shaped the gendered division of productive and reproductive labour across public and private spheres. Domestic worker migration has been associated with the increasing prevalence of female breadwinners who, by virtue of being transnationally separated from the home, are unable to perform gendered care roles associated with parenting and household work (Jayaweera & Dias 2009). As Gamburd (2000) and Lynch (2007) have observed in ethnographic research, this has resulted in the stigmatisation of working women – and increasingly vocal articulations that women should perform the bulk of unpaid care work regardless of their paid work commitments (Rajapaksa 2005; Gunatilaka 2013). In restricting women's foreign employment where migration would impair the performance of unpaid care work, the FBR, therefore, made no attempts to protect women migrant domestic workers but rather reasserted essentialised gender norms embedded in Sri Lankan public discourse and other government policies (Abeyasekera & Jayasundere 2015; Gunaratne 2023). Indeed, evidence suggests the FBR only heightened the risk of harm for women migrant domestic workers by driving stubborn patterns of survival migration into irregular recruitment pathways (Weeraratne 2016; Henderson 2021), ensuring that remittances continue flowing but in lieu of the limited protection offered by regular status.

Myanmar

As discussed in the previous section, Myanmar's recent implementation of migration bans affecting migrant domestic workers appears to have been highly mimetic. The 2014 bans on domestic worker emigration – first to Hong Kong and Singapore, then to all countries – occurred within a few years of similar interventions by other Southeast Asian governments (Napier-Moore 2017) and against the broader policy backdrop of the Philippine Government's pioneering use of retaliatory bans (Shivakoti, Henderson, & Withers 2021). As a fledgling emigration state whose involvement in foreign labour markets is primarily characterised by irregular cross-border flows to Thailand, the benefit of these policies is harder to discern. The Government of Myanmar has 'no bargaining power vis-à-vis receiving states' (Khemanitthathai 2022: 189) with which to enact labour diplomacy, nor any of the accumulated political concerns surrounding women migrant domestic workers, who were only legally permitted to migrate in 2009 and make up a fraction of Myanmar's migration profile (Napier-Moore 2017). Khemanitthathai (2022: 191–192) nonetheless sees Myanmar's initial immigration bans as a genuine attempt to protect women migrant domestic workers from exploitative working conditions, citing evidence that prior opportunities to promote domestic worker emigration to Thailand had been rejected for concern about rights and wages, and noting that the 2014 bans followed high-profile instances of abuse (a catalyst) and the recent publishing of rights-based frameworks drafted in consultation with international organisations (a rationale). In this episode, then, and despite a lack of capacity, the Burmese Government appears to have been exercising pastoral power to safeguard the well-being of women migrant domestic workers who – as in other contexts – have been framed as uniquely vulnerable.

However, the efficacy of the 2014 bans was severely undermined by the prevalence of irregular migration pathways that women could readily access in the absence of state-brokered emigration, and the impetus for subsequent restrictions appears to have shifted towards more instrumental attempts to meet political goals. In striking contrast to the cases of the Philippines and Sri Lanka, though, bans were seemingly not used to win support from the domestic electorate – which remained mired within an uneasy democratic transition from decades of military rule – but to manage external political relations with neighbouring states and exert control over rival political parties. In 2016, several Burmese workers were the victims of violent attacks in Malaysia, which were allegedly acts of revenge in the context of a wider diplomatic breakdown relating to the mistreatment of Rohingya Muslims in Myanmar (Khemanitthathai 2022). In response, Myanmar suspended all migration to Malaysia, citing safety concerns but also broader apprehension that the Malaysian Government's criticism of the plight of Rohingya constituted interference in sovereign political matters that compromised the state's 'external legitimacy' (Khemanitthathai 2022: 196). Later bans implemented during COVID-19 coincided with the resumption of military rule and attempts to use emigration policy, including blacklists on workers who do not sufficiently remit through official state channels, as a means of raising state revenue and defunding nascent democracy movements reliant on remittances (Zin 2022). In both of these latter instances, restrictive emigration policy has again hinged on efforts to preserve state legitimacy – not by meaningfully protecting workers or arbitrating gender norms for political gain, but by aspiring to bolster the symbolic and material basis of frail regimes facing external and internal criticism.

Samoa

Temporary labour migration from Samoa, as with other South Pacific countries participating in labour mobility schemes to Australia and New Zealand, differs from the previous cases in that it is *not* highly feminised. Seasonal labour migration schemes have consistently had upward of 80 per cent male participation, while an initial emphasis on gender equitable participation in Australia's longer-term guestworker scheme was soon abandoned as meat processing became the central industry driving recruitment (Petrou & Withers 2024). Though specific concerns relating to the safety of women migrants do exist, particularly with regard to the suitability of accommodation and incidence of gender-based violence (Kanan & Putt 2022), Samoa has yet to implement gender-based emigration restrictions comparable to the migration bans experienced by women domestic workers in other contexts. However, the zero-tolerance policy of 'standing down' and 'blacklisting' workers has been a core component of Samoa's emigration governance since the formulation of its first Labour Migration Policy in 2014 and how these disciplinary measures have been used reflect the influence of domestic gender politics. The initial rationale for blacklisting was more closely aligned with harnessing the economic benefits of migration by enforcing behavioural expectations: 'selection and recruitment should not only meet employer goals but also meet Samoa community goals and therefore, for example, workers who fail to contribute back to their communities should not be permitted to return for a further period of employment' (Government of Samoa 2014). In practice, however, blacklisting has also been steered towards the policing of social issues relating to community life and the institution of the family, specifically as a punitive measure used in state arbitration of extramarital affairs (Withers 2022). As a government official explained during a prior study, 'Samoa cannot tolerate men – married men – having affairs when they go overseas under different schemes . . . should anything happen like that, the only solution is to return the husband back to Samoa' (Withers 2022: 14). These policies have likewise overseen the forcible return of both single and married women who have given birth while working in Australia and New Zealand (Government of Samoa 2022).

Similar to the case of Sri Lanka, these interventions respond to (and attempt to resolve) the moral crises that emerge when widespread emigration disrupts and reconfigures social reproduction and the gender politics that bind it. As guestworker migration has bourgeoned in recent years, so too have concerns about 'broken homes' where remaining female spouses, over-represented in the performance of unpaid care work and under-represented in the labour market, are left socially and economically vulnerable when relationships break down (Withers 2022). Similarly, concerns for the welfare of children living in migrant households or born abroad have captured news headlines. While Samoa had defended its zero-tolerance policy as 'very effective in countering mischief' (Government of Samoa 2017), growing recognition of the prevalence of social problems has since prompted the government to limit participation on the grounds of ensuring enough people remain to serve local community institutions. Though the extra-jurisdictional disciplining of workers may have once been capable of simultaneously producing ideal migrant subjects (to promote further emigration) and addressing growing social concerns (to maintain political legitimacy), it appears as though the sheer scale of emigration has come to erode the base of socially reproductive institutions. In Samoa, such institutions frequently exist outside of capitalist social relations and depend on the reciprocity of unpaid labour that remittances cannot readily compensate for. In response, the state appears to have emboldened its political rhetoric and policy interventions, signalling the intention to circumscribe future participation while strengthening efforts to police workers' behaviour – including the enforcement of mandatory savings schemes and restrictions on the drinking of alcohol (Meleisea 2023).

Beyond Efficacy

In each of the these cases, emigration bans and blacklists can be seen to take shape around a central tension between promoting emigration for economic reasons and constraining certain forms of mobility for political reasons. In most instances, restrictions are explicitly applied to the mobility of working-class women, whose assumed vulnerability has been mediated and politicised as a matter requiring state intervention. In the outlying case of Samoa, blacklists have been more readily used to sanction men accused of neglecting familial roles and responsibilities, allegedly threatening the welfare of women who *remain,* but have also been used to control the circumstances of biological reproduction by recalling pregnant women workers. These examples offer distinctive explanations for the 'unresolved paradox' of migration bans that together dispute the generalisability of the Philippine Government's inclination towards the exercise of pastoral power to cultivate 'self-advocating subjects' and thereby afford protection (Parreñas 2021). For other emigration states, bans enacted in the name of protecting women have often done little to improve welfare outcomes; their efficacy in enhancing the conditions of temporary labour migration is chronically undermined by a lack of bargaining power and the prevalence of irregular pathways that circumvent formal restrictions (Lenard 2021). These limitations pervade even the 'best practice' case of the Philippines. When the first unilateral ban was enforced in 1988, several destination countries responded immediately, signing bilateral agreements defining minimum protections; some retaliated by placing an embargo on the recruitment of all Filipino workers, thus placing economic pressure on the Philippines' nascent remittance economy. Meanwhile, others – including most GCC countries – simply recruited more workers from other countries (Henderson 2021). Other accounts indicate that workers readily circumvented the bans, either engaging recruiters from third countries where restrictions were not enforced (Parreñas 2015) or travelling irregularly on tourist visas (Shah 1991).

The ad hoc and ever more frequent use of migration bans and blacklists by individual emigration states, despite the mounting evidence of their inefficacy in stemming migration or procuring BLAs, troubles the notion that the protection of migrant workers is an overarching objective of these policies. Indeed, the persistent absence of coordinated multilateral bargaining by prominent emigration states in the Asia-Pacific region, which would foreseeably provide a more effective platform for demanding improved rights and conditions within specific foreign labour markets, points to divergent self-interest among governments vying to promote further emigration under competitive circumstances. The preceding analysis instead suggests that migration bans are better understood as inward-facing policies that capitalise on the political value of symbolic interventions that address social and cultural dilemmas emerging from the contradictions inherent to remittance economies. Importantly, these conspicuous acts of state power most often demonstrate a decoupling of the interests held by emigration states and migrant workers, as the latter are seldom key political constituents. The Philippines is here an exception, owing to the deliberate promotion of transnational citizenship and migrant political representation as a means of tethering a vast global diaspora to the remittance economy (Rodriguez 2002). It is perhaps unsurprising, therefore, that Parreñas (2021) observes the 'disciplining and empowerment' of Filipina migrant domestic workers – whereas, in Sri Lanka, restrictions have appealed to a more politically salient undercurrent of patriarchal ethnonationalism; in Myanmar, they have morphed into attempts to reinforce the authority of embattled regimes; and in Samoa, they have been used to police the moral values that sustain cultural institutions of political importance. If seen as symbolic action in response to contextually specific concerns, rather than protection measures per se, these policies find a common explanation in their intended political utility.

It is not coincidental that, despite their distinctive characteristics, these interventions collectively situate gender norms and women's bodies as sites of political and economic tension. Emigration states here echo a longer tradition of 'body politics' in development (Harcourt 2009), whereby 'othered' bodies become, physically and normatively, sites of political contestation over the denial and realisation of rights. This section has shown that women have been alternately constructed – as empowered and vulnerable, independent and dependent, productive and reproductive – depending on whether they are being celebrated as economic breadwinners or paternalised as literal and metaphorical 'reproducers of the nation' (de Alwis 1996). Between these extremes lie what appear to be genuine attempts to improve the rights and working conditions of women whose circumstances of foreign employment are, in many cases, objectively worse than their male counterparts – though the dubious efficacy of bans raises questions about the sincerity of these measures beyond the spectacle of state action. Across all cases though, it has reaffirmed that the contested domain of gender norms is a potent site for the political imaginary of emigration states and suggested that, while remittance economies are characterised by multiple contradictions, it is perhaps the slower-burning crises of social reproduction that are ultimately the most profound (Triandafyllidou *et al.* 2024: 10).

Conclusion: From Developmental to Emigration States

This Element has brought together and sought to reconcile questions that have animated a decade of research into the political economy of temporary labour migration across the Asia-Pacific region. In many ways, its germination can be traced to a single moment when I attended a migration policy symposium in Colombo in 2014. Consecutive government presentations first outlined the need to upskill and protect women migrant domestic workers in the wake of Rizana Nafeek's execution the previous year and then offered a labour market analysis identifying promising demand for domestic work in Saudi Arabia – the very country in which Nafeek was killed. Struck by the incoherence of these policy rationales, it occurred to me that the contradictions I was then observing in the structure of Sri Lanka's remittance economy were mirrored in the way governments tasked themselves, politically, with managing opposing pressures to constrain and promote further emigration. My thesis, however, continued to elaborate on the economic aspects of this dilemma – identifying overlapping path dependencies on migration and remittances at multiple scales to connect household finances to local economies, national accounting, and regional patterns of uneven development (Withers 2019b). It was not until later research into restrictions placed on the emigration of Sri Lankan women migrant domestic workers (Withers 2019a) – and collaborations enabling comparative analysis of these policies in India, Indonesia, Nepal, and the Philippines (Shivakoti, Henderson, & Withers 2021; Joseph *et al.* 2022) – that it became clear that the politicisation of women's bodies and the reproductive labour they disproportionately perform was central to the governance of remittance economies. This impression was further affirmed by research at the outset of Australia's PLS, when interviews with I-Kiribati, ni-Vanuatu and Tongan workers – and, later, government officials from Fiji, Samoa, Tonga, and Vanuatu (Withers 2022) – revealed a common concern that income gains were being offset by the broader social consequences of transnational family separation and the breakdown of personal and community ties (Withers 2024).

Emerging from this expanding research agenda was a need to coherently explain, in comparative perspective, the connections between the common material basis of remittance economies and the varying political logics of emigration states that govern them. Prominent accounts within the existing migration literature appeared to have stopped short of fully reconciling these political and economic factors. On the one hand, perspectives emphasising the developmental motivations of emigration states have downplayed the complexity of remittance-dependent economies by typologising labour brokerage states as a subcategory of emigration states whose political and economic imperatives are rendered overly homogenous (Gamlen 2019; Adamson & Tsourapas 2020). Inattentive – as typologies necessarily are – to the particular histories, economic geographies, and social realities of remittance economies and the foreign labour markets they are connected to, these analyses risk flattening the nuance and specificity of emigration policymaking. On the other hand, accounts that afford greater attention to the complexity of emigration governance, whether focussing on a single state (Rodriguez 2002; Tyner 2010; Parreñas 2021) or offering comparative analysis (Oishi 2005; Ireland 2018; Shivakoti, Henderson, & Withers 2021), have tended to advance an understanding of political tensions fomenting at the surface, rather than the root, of remittance economies. The deeper path dependencies and opportunity costs of now-foreclosed developmental alternatives, and the historical structures of uneven development that have shaped these eventualities, often remain unexamined. This Element has primarily been an attempt to bridge these approaches – the developmental and the governmental – to provide a more compelling account of emigration policymaking across Asia-Pacific contexts where guestwork has become entrenched as a driving force of social and economic life.

The starting point for this analysis was to reconsider the migration-development nexus with greater attentiveness to concerns surrounding agrarian transition and industrialisation that were foundational to early debates but have since been decentred. Adopting a historical-structural approach, *Section 1* emphasised the continuing salience of constraints and challenges identified by pioneering contributions in the field of developmental economics: the imbalanced terms of trade between core and peripheral economies and the difficulty of aligning labour migration with industrial policy. For those economies unable to find a footing on the ladder of industrial development – many having had only a brief window of opportunity for 'catching up' between colonial occupation and postcolonial debt crises – international labour migration and the remittances it generates was seen to offer a largely cosmetic resolution to the persistent challenges posed by domestic unemployment and balance of payments issues. It was argued that the now commonplace strategy of pursuing 'migration instead of development' has failed to deliver the developmental benefits anticipated by a reductive triple-win agenda that is still echoed throughout national, regional, and global policy rhetoric. Instead, it was determined that remittance economies are structurally undermined by three central contradictions. Firstly, large remittance transfers have important macroeconomic implications beyond the short-term benefits conferred to national accounting and household expenditure, leading to currency appreciation (that undermines the competitiveness of export industries) and stimulating import expenditure (that worsens existing trade deficits). Secondly, labour-sending states are incentivised to promote further migration rather than confront growing obstacles to industrial policy and local job creation, undermining commitments to inclusive development and decent work. Thirdly, the transnational family separation that guestworker migration routinely involves has substantial implications for households and communities to socially reproduce current and future generations. Staving off these looming contradictions, it is argued, becomes a central policy focus of emigration states.

In *Section 2*, these economic contradictions were more explicitly linked to policy interventions to advance an understanding of the imperatives and strategies that characterise emigration governance. By surveying the migration patterns and policy histories of four distinct emigration states in the Asia-Pacific region – Myanmar, the Philippines, Samoa, and Sri Lanka – it was shown that there are clear commonalities in the way governments engage in labour brokerage, create regulatory institutions in response to the concerns of workers and families, and act with urgency when migration-related crises arise. However, it likewise exposed crucial differences in how emigration states designed and implemented policies over time, reflective of differing modalities and rationalities of governance. These differences were further explored through the adoption of a Foucauldian lens of governmentality, which afforded a more detailed analysis of the way states and responsibilised non-state actors co-constitute frameworks through which migration is promoted, mediated, and conserved. The ensuing analysis exposed multiple registers of meaning and degrees of policy efficacy across the four countries in question, reflecting the contextual specificity of social relations within each emigration state but also an overarching tension between competing economic and political logics more generally. It was argued that emigration must be at once promoted and constrained, requiring the responsibilisation of self-governing subjects motivated to migrate and remit, but also conspicuous – if largely symbolic – acts of state intervention regarding issues of public concern.

The competing objectives of promoting migration for economic purposes while constraining migration for political purposes were further explored in *Section 3*, which addressed the implementation of emigration bans that primarily affect the mobility of women migrant domestic workers. This final section situates female bodies and women's socially reproductive labour as a site of policy intervention and considers the differing rationales through which emigration states have implemented and justified bans and blacklists that have limited capacity to restrict movement but carry decisive political value. The analysis is framed in reply to Parreñas's (2021) interrogation of these policies in the case of the Philippines, where the routine implementation of bans is understood as reflective of the state's conflicting compulsions to promote and protect women migrant domestic workers in order to sustain a developmental strategy hinging on labour export. While Parreñas's conclusions are not contested, their generalisability is. By considering countervailing examples in Sri Lanka (where the restriction of women's migration is more readily linked to affirming patriarchal care norms), Myanmar (where state fragility has impeded and co-opted the rationale of protection), and Samoa (where blacklisting explicitly attempts to police moral values and cultural institutions), it is instead argued that bans arise in response to meet a plurality of political objectives beyond 'protection'.

The central contribution of this Element, brought together across these three sections, has thus been to extend connections between the developmental challenges faced by remittance economies and the complex political terrain of emigration policymaking. It has shown that the four emigration states examined exhibit coherence in a shared strategy of 'migration instead of development' that circumvents some of the economic challenges encountered in earlier decades but that this transition – from developmental to emigration states – has likewise necessitated new modes of governance. Political legitimacy, once rooted in the capability of governments to oversee development *in situ*, has significantly shifted towards the ability to responsibilise self-governing migrant households and periodically puncture this outsourcing of accountability with symbolic interventions that have frequently reified women's bodies as sites of material and ideological contestation. Nonetheless, the varied 'fixes' of emigration governance represent an unsustainable compromise that fails to deviate from the underlying political-economic realities of brokering labour to subsidise the production and social reproduction of foreign economies. Indeed, though it was originally planned to conclude this Element with a more hopeful discussion of 'roadmaps through the remittance trap', this prospect seems palpably naive in light of a fresh coup in Myanmar, the collapse of Sri Lanka's remittance economy, brewing political crises concerning the social impacts of migration in

Samoa, and the newly elected government of Marcos Jr seemingly redoubling the Philippines's integration within foreign labour markets. Instead, recent events have only underscored the fragility of remittance economies and highlighted the need for greater academic and policymaking engagement with emigration governance as a complex and contested domain that is as much inward-looking as it is concerned with conditions prevailing in foreign labour markets.

Emigration states are instrumental, if frequently misunderstood, stakeholders in the temporary labour migration schemes that now undergird the political economy of the Asia-Pacific region. A greater attentiveness to their commonalities (which are not as uniform as recent typologies might suggest) and differences (which are not as pronounced as other accounts sometimes imply) can aspire to a better understanding of the political and economic motives of those governing remittance-dependent economies. This, in turn, could foreseeably foster opportunities for improved policy learning between emigration states facing similar problems and lay the groundwork for multilateral bargaining that is, more than ever, sorely needed to address the degraded rights and conditions of foreign employment from which so many of the limitations of remittance economies originate.

References

Abeyasekera, A., & Jayasundere, R. (2015). Migrant Mothers, Family Breakdown, and the Modern State: An Analysis of State Policies Regulating Women Migrating Overseas for Domestic Work in Sri Lanka. *The South Asianist*, **4** (1), 1–24.

Abeyasekera, A., Maqsood, A., Perera, I., Sajjad, F., & Spencer, J. (2019). Discipline in Sri Lanka, Punish in Pakistan: Neoliberalism, Governance, and Housing Compared. *Journal of the British Academy*, **7**(2), 215–244.

Abeysinghe, A. (20 September 2023). Wickremesinghe: Industrialized Countries Compensate for 'Brain Drain'. *AsiaNews*, Sri Lanka. www.asianews.it/news-en/Wickremesinghe:-industrialized-countries-compensate-for-'brain-drain'-59190.html.

Adamson, F. B., Chung, E. A., & Hollifield, J. F. (2024). Rethinking the Migration State: Historicising, Decolonising, and Disaggregating. *Journal of Ethnic and Migration Studies*, **50**(3), 559–577.

Adamson, F. B., & Tsourapas, G. (2020). The Migration State in the Global South: Nationalizing, Developmental, and Neoliberal Models of Migration Management. *International Migration Review*, **54**(3), 853–882.

Agarwala, R. (2022). *The Migration-Development Regime: How Class Shapes Indian Emigration*, New York: Oxford University Press. https://doi.org/10.1093/oso/9780197586396.001.0001.

Agunias, D. R., & Ruiz, N. G. (2007). *Protecting Overseas Workers: Lessons and Cautions from the Philippines*, Washington DC: Migration Policy Institute.

Ahlburg, D. A. (1991). *Remittances and their Impact: A Study of Tonga and Western Samoa*, Canberra: National Centre for Development Studies, Research School of Pacific Studies, the Australian National University.

Ahlin, T. (2018). Only Near Is Dear? Doing Elderly Care with Everyday ICTs in Indian Transnational Families: Elderly Care with ICTs in Indian Families. *Medical Anthropology Quarterly*, **32**(1), 85–102.

Akee, R., & Kapur, D. (2017). *Myanmar Remittances* (No. S-53405-MYA-1), International Growth Centre. Retrieved from https://www.theigc.org/sites/default/files/2018/06/Akee-and-Kapur-2017-Final-report.pdf.

Alipio, C. (2019). Lives Lived in 'Someone Else's Hands': Precarity and Profit-Making of Migrants and Left-Behind Children in the Philippines. *TRaNS: Trans-Regional and National Studies of Southeast Asia*, **7**(1), 135–158.

Andriesse, E. (2018). Primary Sector Value Chains, Poverty Reduction, and Rural Development Challenges in the Philippines. *Geographical Review,* **108** (3), 345–366.

Angenendt, S. (2014). *Creating a Triple-Win through Labor Migration Policy? Lessons from Germany* (Framework Paper), Washington, DC: The German Marshall Fund.

Arambepola, C. (2023). Casting Outside Regular Pathways: State Restrictions to Sri Lankan Female Migration. In I. van Liempt, J. Schapendonk, & A. Campos-Delgado, eds., *Research Handbook on Irregular Migration,* Northampton: Edward Elgar, pp. 227–237.

Baey, G., & Yeoh, B. S. (2015). Migration and Precarious Work: Negotiating Debt, Employment, and Livelihood Strategies amongst Bangladeshi Migrant Men Working in Singapore's Construction Industry. *Migrating Out of Poverty Working Paper,* **26**, 1–36.

Baldassar, L., Baldock, C. V., & Wilding, R. (2007). *Families Caring across Borders,* London: Palgrave Macmillan UK. https://doi.org/10.1057/9780230626263.

Barajas, A., Chami, R., Fullenkamp, C., & Montiel, P. (2009). *Do Workers' Remittances Promote Economic Growth?* (Working Paper No. WP/09/153), Washington DC: International Monetary Fund (IMF).

Battistella, G. (2012). Multi-level Policy Approach in the Governance of Labour Migration: Considerations from the Philippine Experience. *Asian Journal of Social Science,* **40**(4), 419–446.

Bauböck, R., & Ruhs, M. (2022). The Elusive Triple Win: Addressing Temporary Labour Migration Dilemmas through Fair Representation. *Migration Studies,* **10**(3), 528–552, mnac021.

Bertram, G. (2006). Introduction: The MIRAB Model in the Twenty-First Century. *Asia Pacific Viewpoint,* **47**(1), 1–13.

Bhattacharya, T. (2017). Mapping Social Reproduction Theory. In T. Bhattacharya, & L. Vogel, eds., *Social Reproduction Theory: Remapping Class, Recentering Oppression,* London: Pluto Press, pp. 1–20.

Binford, L. (2003). Migrant Remittances and (Under)Development in Mexico. *Critique of Anthropology,* **23**(3), 305–336.

Bonacich, E. (1972). A Theory of Ethnic Antagonism: The Split Labor Market. *American Sociological Review,* **37**(5), 547.

Boucher, A., & Gest, J. (2015). Migration Studies at a Crossroads: A Critique of Immigration Regime Typologies. *Migration Studies,* **3**(2), 182–198.

Breman, J. (2010). *Outcast Labour in Asia: Circulation and Informalization of the Workforce at the Bottom of the Economy,* New Delhi: Oxford University Press.

Brown, R. P. C., & Ahlburg, D. A. (1999). Remittances in the South Pacific. *International Journal of Social Economics*, **26**(1/2/3), 325–344.

Burawoy, M. (1976). The Functions and Reproduction of Migrant Labor: Comparative Material from Southern Africa and the United States. *American Journal of Sociology*, **81**(5), 1050–1087.

Cabalquinto, E. C. B. (2022). *(Im)mobile Homes: Family Life at a Distance in the Age of Mobile Media*, First ed, New York: Oxford University Press.

Campbell, I. (2019). Harvest Labour Markets in Australia: Alleged Labour Shortages and Employer Demand for Temporary Migrant Workers. *Journal of Australian Political Economy*, **43**, 46–88.

Castles, S. (2010). Understanding Global Migration: A Social Transformation Perspective. *Journal of Ethnic and Migration Studies*, **36**(10), 1565–1586.

Chami, R., Ernst, E., Fullenkamp, C., & Oeking, A. (2018). *Is There a Remittance Trap?*, Washington DC: International Monetary Fund (IMF).

Chan, C. (2014). Gendered Morality and Development Narratives: The Case of Female Labor Migration from Indonesia. *Sustainability*, **6**(10), 6949–6972.

Chang, A. S. (2018). Producing the Self-Regulating Subject: Liberal Protection in Indonesia's Migration Infrastructure. *Pacific Affairs*, **91**(4), 695–716.

Chang, H.-J. (2003). *Kicking Away the Ladder Development Strategy in Historical Perspective*, London: Anthem Press.

Chi, X. (2008). Challenging Managed Temporary Labor Migration as a Model for Rights and Development for Labor-Sending Countries. *New York University Journal of International Law and Politics*, **40**, 497–540.

Chopra, D., & Sweetman, C. (2014). Introduction to Gender, Development and Care. *Gender & Development*, **22**(3), 409–421.

Chua, K. K., Limkin, L., Nye, J., & Williamson, J. G. (2015). Urban-Rural Income and Wage Gaps in the Philippines: Measurement Error, Unequal Endowments, or Factor Market Failure?, *Philippine Review of Economics*, **52**(2), 1–21.

Chung, E., Draudt, D., & Tian, Y. (2024). The Developmental Migration State. *Journal of Ethnic and Migration Studies*, **50**(3), 637–656.

Chung, E., Hollifield, J. F., & Tian, Y. (2023). Migration Governance in East and Southeast Asia. *International Relations of the Asia-Pacific*, **24**(3), 497–522, lcad010.

Cohen, R. (1987). *The New Helots: Migrants in the International Division of Labour*, Aldershot: Brookfield.

Collins, J. L. (1991). Women and the Environment: Social Reproduction and Sustainable Development. In R. S. Gallin, & A. Ferguson, eds., *The Women and International Development Annual*, 1st ed, London: Routledge, pp. 33–58.

Connell, J. (1983). *Migration, Employment and Development in the South Pacific* (Country Report No. 22), Noumea: South Pacific Commission.

Connell, J., & Brown, R. P. C. (2005). Remittances in the Pacific: An Overview, Manila: Asian Development Bank.

Craven, L. K. (2015). Migration-Affected Change and Vulnerability in Rural Vanuatu. *Asia Pacific Viewpoint*, **56**(2), 223–236.

Crawley, H., & Teye, J. K. (Eds.). (2024). *The Palgrave Handbook of South–South Migration and Inequality*, Cham: Springer. https://doi.org/10.1007/978-3-031-39814-8.

Dahinden, J., Fischer, C., & Menet, J. (2021). Knowledge Production, Reflexivity, and the Use of Categories in Migration Studies: Tackling Challenges in the Field. *Ethnic and Racial Studies*, **44**(4), 535–554.

Das, M., & N'Diaye, P. (2013). *Chronicle of a Decline Foretold: Has China Reached the Lewis Turning Point?* (No. WP/13/26), Washington DC: International Monetary Fund (IMF).

de Alwis, M. (1996). Gender, Politics and the 'Respectable Lady'. In P. Jeganathan, & Q. Ismail, eds., *Unmakng the Nation: The Politics of Identity and History in Modern Sri Lanka*, Colombo: Social Scientists' Association, pp. 137–157.

de Haas, H. (2010). Migration and Development: A Theoretical Perspective. *International Migration Review*, **44**(1), 227–264.

de Haas, H. (2012). The Migration and Development Pendulum: A Critical View on Research and Policy: The Migration and Development Pendulum. *International Migration*, **50**(3), 8–25.

Delgado Wise, R. (2009). Forced Migration and US Imperialism: The Dialectic of Migration and Development. *Critical Sociology*, **35**(6), 767–784.

Deshingkar, P. (2021). Criminalisation of Migration for Domestic Work from Myanmar to Singapore – Need for a Radical Policy Shift. *European Journal on Criminal Policy and Research*. https://doi.org/10.1007/s10610-020-09477-w.

Deshingkar, P., Abrar, C. R., Sultana, M. T., Haque, K. N. H., & Reza, M. S. (2018). Producing Ideal Bangladeshi Migrants for Precarious Construction Work in Qatar. *Journal of Ethnic and Migration Studies*, **45**(14), 2723–2738.

Doan, D., Dornan, M., & Edwards, R. (2023). *The Gains and Pains of Working Away from Home*, Suva: World Bank.

Droessler, H. (2018). Copra World: Coconuts, Plantations and Cooperatives in German Samoa. *The Journal of Pacific History*, **53**(4), 417–435.

Dziedzic, S., Voloder, D., & Raela, J. (30 August 2023). Pacific Countries Are Not 'outposts' to Grow Labourers for Australia, Samoan PM says. *ABC*

News. www.abc.net.au/news/2023-08-31/fiame-samoa-pacific-labour-scheme-australia/102794256.

Eelens, F., Mook, T., & Schampers, T. (1992). Introduction. In F. Eelens, T. Schampers, & J. D. Speckermann, eds., *Labour Migration to the Middle East: From Sri Lanka to the Gulf*, London: Kegan Paul International, pp. 1–27.

Eelens, F., & Speckmann, J. D. (1992). Recruitment of Labour Migrants for the Middle East. In F. Eelens, T. Schampers, & J. D. Speckermann, eds., *Labour Migration to the Middle East: From Sri Lanka to the Gulf*, London: Kegan Paul International, pp. 41–62.

Elson, D., & Pearson, R. (1981). 'Nimble Fingers Make Cheap Workers': An Analysis of Women's Employment in Third World Export Manufacturing. *Feminist Review*, 7(Spring), 87–107.

Eversole, R., & Shaw, J. (2010). Remittance Flows and Their Use in Households: A Comparative Study of Sri Lanka, Indonesia and the Philippines. *Asian and Pacific Migration Journal*, **19**(2), 175–202.

Faier, L. (2013). Affective Investments in the Manila Region: Filipina Migrants in Rural Japan and Transnational Urban Development in the Philippines. *Transactions of the Institute of British Geographers*, **38**(3), 376–390.

Faist, T. (2008). Migrants as Transnational Development Agents: An Inquiry into the Newest Round of the Migration–Development Nexus. *Population, Space and Place*, **14**(1), 21–42.

Faist, T., & Fauser, M. (2011). The Migration–Development Nexus: Toward a Transnational Perspective. In T. Faist, M. Fauser, & P. Kivisto, eds., *The Migration-Development Nexus*, London: Palgrave Macmillan UK, pp. 1–26.

Feagaimaali'i, J., & Fotheringham, C. (3 February 2023). Workers Prepare to Head Overseas After Samoa Lifts RSE Suspension. www.rnz.co.nz/international/pacific-news/483561/workers-prepare-to-head-overseas-after-samoa-lifts-rse-suspension.

Ferguson, J., & Gupta, A. (2002). Spatializing States: Toward an Ethnography of Neoliberal Governmentality. *American Ethnologist*, **29**(4), 981–1002.

Fiddian-Qasmiyeh, E. (2024). Recentring the South in Studies of Migration. In H. Crawley & J. K. Teye, eds., *The Palgrave Handbook of South–South Migration and Inequality*, Cham: Springer, pp. 47–73.

Fitzgerald, D. (2006). Inside the Sending State: The Politics of Mexican Emigration Control. *International Migration Review*, **40**(2), 259–293.

Foucault, M. (1991). Governmentality. In G. Burchell, C. Gordon, & P. Miller, eds., *The Foucault Effect: Studies in Governmentality: With Two Lectures by and an Interview with Michel Foucault*, Chicago: University of Chicago Press, pp. 87–104.

Fraser, N. (1997). *Justice Interruptus: Critical Reflections on the 'Postsocialist' Condition*, New York: Routledge.

Gamburd, M. R. (2000). *The Kitchen Spoon's Handle: Transnationalism and Sri Lanka's Migrant Housemaids*, Ithaca: Cornell University Press.

Gamburd, M. R. (2009). Advocating for Sri Lankan Migrant Workers: Obstacles and Challenges. *Critical Asian Studies*, **41**(1), 61–88.

Gamlen, A. (2014). Diaspora Institutions and Diaspora Governance. *International Migration Review*, **48**(1_suppl), 180–217.

Gamlen, A. (2019). Labour Export from the Asian Body Shops. In A. Gamlen, *Human Geopolitics*, Oxford: Oxford University Press, pp. 106–124.

Gazzotti, L., Mouthaan, M., & Natter, K. (2023). Embracing Complexity in 'Southern' Migration Governance. *Territory, Politics, Governance*, **11**(4), 625–637.

Ghosh, J. (2019). A Brave New World, or the Same Old Story with New Characters? *Development and Change*, **50**(2), 379–393.

Glenn, E. N. (1992). From Servitude to Service Work: Historical Continuities in the Racial Division of Paid Reproductive Labor. *Signs: Journal of Women in Culture and Society*, **18**(1), 1–43.

Gonzalez, J. J. (1998). *Philippine Labour Migration: Critical Dimensions of Public Policy*, Singapore: Institute of Southeast Asian Studies.

Government of Samoa. (2014). *Samoa Labour Mobility Policy – Consultation Paper*. www.samoagovt.ws/wp-content/uploads/2014/12/Samoa-LMP-Consultation-Paper-FINAL-1.pdf.

Government of Samoa. (6 July 2017). Hon. Lautafi Fio Selafi Purcell's Address for the RSE Employers Conference, Facebook.

Government of Samoa. (2022). *Samoa National Employment Policy (SNEP-2) 2021–2026*, Apia, Samoa: Ministry of Commerce, Industry and Labour. www.mcil.gov.ws/wp-content/uploads/2022/11/SNEP-2021.22-2025 .26_Final.pdf.

Graves, A. (1986). Colonialism and Indentured Labour Migration in the Western Pacific, 1840–1915. In P. C. Emmer, ed., *Colonialism and Migration; Indentured Labour before and after Slavery*, Dordrecht: Springer Netherlands, pp. 237–259.

Guevarra, A. R. (2010). *Marketing Dreams, Manufacturing Heroes: The Transnational Labor Brokering of Filipino Workers*, New Brunswick: Rutgers University Press.

Guevarra, A. R. (2014). Supermaids: The Racial Branding of Global Filipino Care Labour. In B. Anderson & I. Shutes, eds., *Migration and Care Labour*, London: Palgrave Macmillan UK, pp. 130–150.

Gunaratne, J. (2023). Gendered State: 'Governmentality' and the Labour Migration Policy of Sri Lanka. *Sri Lanka Journal of Social Sciences*, **46** (1), 65–80.

Gunatilaka, R. (2013). *Women's Participation in Sri Lanka's Labour Force: Trends, Drivers and Constraints*, Colombo: International Labour Organisation.

Gunatilleke, G., Colombage, S. S., & Perera, M. (2010). *Macroeconomic Impact of International Migration: A Case Study of Sri Lanka* (No. 10–06), Colombo: MARGA.

Haan, A. de. (2006). *Migration in the Development Studies Literature: Has It Come Out of Its Marginality?* WIDER Research Paper, No. 2006/19, ISBN 9291907871, The United Nations University World Institute for Development Economics Research (UNU-WIDER), Helsinki (Working Paper).

Haas, H. de. (2023). *How Migration Really Works: A Factful Guide to the Most Divisive Issue in Politics*, London: Viking.

Hahamovitch, C. (2003). Creating Perfect Immigrants: Guestworkers of the World in Historical Perspective. *Labor History*, **44**(1), 69–94.

Handapangoda, W. S. (2024). The Making of '*Passengers*': The Pre-departure Subjectivation of Sri Lanka's Aspiring Migrant Domestic Workers Heading to the Arabian Gulf. *Global Society*, **38**(2), 248–268.

Harcourt, W. (2009). *Body Politics in Development: Critical Debates in Gender and Development*, London: ZedBooks.

Henderson, S. (2021). *Protecting the Rights of Women Migrant Domestic Workers: Structural Violence and Competing Interests in the Philippines and Sri Lanka*, 1st ed, London: Routledge. https://doi.org/10.4324/9781003179085.

Hickel, J. (2017). Is Global Inequality Getting Better or Worse? A Critique of the World Bank's Convergence Narrative. *Third World Quarterly*, **38**(10), 2208–2222.

Hill, E., & Palit, A. (Eds.). (2018). *Employment Policy in Emerging Economies: The Indian Case*, London: Routledge, Taylor & Francis Group.

Ho, S. P. (2008). Arguing for Policy Space to Promote Development: Prebisch, Myrdal, and Singer. *Journal of Economic Issues*, **XLII**(2), 509–516.

Hoang, L. A. (2017). Governmentality in Asian Migration Regimes: The Case of Labour Migration from Vietnam to Taiwan: Governmentality in Labour Migration from Vietnam to Taiwan. *Population, Space and Place*, **23**(3), e2019.

Hollifield, J. F. (1992). *Immigrants, Markets, and States: The Political Economy of Postwar Europe*, Cambridge, MA: Harvard University Press.

Hollifield, J. F. (2004). The Emerging Migration State. *International Migration Review*, **38**(3), 885–912.

Hughes, H., & Sodhi, G. (2006). *Should Australia and New Zealand Open Their Doors to Guest Workers From the Pacific? Costs and Benefits* (No. 72), Centre for Independent Studies (CIS).

Hwang, M. C. (2018). Gendered Border Regimes and Displacements: The Case of Filipina Sex Workers in Asia. *Signs: Journal of Women in Culture and Society*, **43**(3), 515–537.

ILO. (2015). *Review of the Effectiveness of the MOUs in Managing Labour Migration between Thailand and Neighbouring Countries*, Bangkok, Thailand: ILO Regional Office for Asia and the Pacific. www.ilo.org/wcmsp5/groups/public/–asia/–ro-bangkok/documents/publication/wcms_356542.pdf.

Institute of Policy Studies (IPS). (2014). *Summary Report: International Conference on Policies for Mainstreaming Migration into Development in Sri Lanka, 14 August 2014*, Colombo: Institute of Policy Studies of Sri Lanka.

International Labour Organisation. (2020). *Female Labour Migration from Pakistan: A Situation Analysis*, Geneva: International Labour Organisation. www.ilo.org/wcmsp5/groups/public/–ed_protect/–protrav/–migrant/documents/publication/wcms_735795.pdf.

International Labour Organisation (ILO). (2018). *Sri Lankan Female Migrant Workers and the Family Background Report*, Colombo, Sri Lanka: International Labour Organisation (ILO). www.ilo.org/wcmsp5/groups/public/–asia/–ro-bangkok/–ilo-colombo/documents/publication/wcms_632484.pdf.

International Organization for Migration (IOM). (2013). *Crushed Hopes: Underemployment and Deskilling among Skilled Migrant Women*, International Organisation for Migration. https://doi.org/10.18356/7eff69cf-en.

International Organization for Migration (IOM). (2023). National Reintegration Center for OFWs | Migrants in Countries in Crisis (MICIC). https://micicinitiative.iom.int/national-reintegration-center-ofws.

Ireland, P. R. (2018). The Limits of Sending-State Power: The Philippines, Sri Lanka, and Female Migrant Domestic Workers. *International Political Science Review*, **39**(3), 322–337.

Irudaya Rajan, S., & Joseph, J. (2015). Migrant Women at the Discourse-Policy Nexus: Indian Domestic Workers in Saudi Arabia. In S. Irudaya Rajan, ed., *Gender and Migration*, New Delhi: Routledge, pp. 9–25.

Jayaweera, S., & Dias, M. (2009). Gender Roles and Support Networks of Spouses of Migrant Workers. In *Gender and Labour Migration in Asia*, IOM International Organization for Migration, pp. 43–115.

Jessop, B. (2016). *The State: Past, Present, Future*, Malden, MA: Polity Press.

Jirattikorn, A. (2015). *Managing Migration in Myanmar and Thailand: Economic Reforms, Policies, Practices and Challenges*, Singapore: ISEAS.

Johnson, C. (1982). *MITI and the Japanese Miracle: The Growth of Industrial Policy, 1925–1975*, Stanford, CA: Stanford University Press. www.loc.gov/catdir/toc/cam027/81051330.html.

Jones, K., Ksaifi, L., & Clark, C. (2022). 'The Biggest Problem We Are Facing Is the Running Away Problem': Recruitment and the Paradox of Facilitating the Mobility of Immobile Workers. *Work, Employment and Society*, 095001702210947.

Joseph, J., Henderson, S., Withers, M., & Shivakoti, R. (2022). Regulation through Responsibilisation: Gendered Exit Policies and Precarious Migration from India and Sri Lanka. *International Migration*, imig.13074.

Kanan, L., & Putt, D. J. (2022). Safety and Wellbeing in the PALM Scheme, Presented at the Australasian AID Conference, Canberra, Australia.

Kaur, A. (2004). *Wage Labour in Southeast Asia since 1840 Globalization, the International Division of Labour and Labour Transformations*, Basingstoke: Palgrave Macmillan.

Kelegama, S. (2006). *Development under Stress: Sri Lankan Economy in Transition*, New Delhi: Sage Publications.

Keresoma, L. (21 September 2022). Four Liaison Officers Approved for Seasonal Workers Program. https://talamua.com/2022/09/22/four-liaison-officers-approved-for-seasonal-workers-program/.

Khemanitthathai, S. (2022). *Emigration State in Transition: Foreign Policy Goals in Myanmar's Emigration Policies and Practices*, School of Oriental and African Studies, University of London. https://eprints.soas.ac.uk/id/eprint/37407.

King, R. (2012). *Theories and Typologies of Migration: An Overview and a Primer*, Malmö: Malmö University.

Klotz, A. (2024). Imperial Migration States. *Journal of Ethnic and Migration Studies*, **50**(3), 578–596.

Kofman, E., & Raghuram, P. (2009). *Skiilled Female Labour Migration* (Policy Brief No. 13), Hamburg: Hamburgisches WeltWirtschafts Institut. http://focus-migration.hwwi.de/typo3_upload/groups/3/focus_Migration_Publikationen/Kurzdossiers/PB_13_skilled_fem_l_m.pdf.

Kofman, E., & Raghuram, P. (2015). *Gendered Migrations and Global Social Reproduction*, Basingstoke: Palgrave Macmillan. www.myilibrary.com?id=760666.

Kottegoda, S. (2004). *Negotiating Household Politics: Women's Strategies in Urban Sri Lanka*, Colombo: Social Scientists' Association.

Kuptsch, C. (Ed.). (2006). *Merchants of Labour*, Geneva: International Labour Organisation (ILO).

Kusakabe, K., & Pearson, R. (2010). Transborder Migration, Social Reproduction and Economic Development: A Case Study of Burmese Women Workers in Thailand: Burmese Women Workers in Thailand. *International Migration*, **48** (6), 13–43.

Lacroix, T. (2022). The Transnational State and Migration: Reach, Flows and Policies. *Political Geography*, **94**, 102571.

Lafoai, J. (14 January 2021). 'Your Attitude will Determine Your Success' – PM to RSE Workers. *Samoa Global News*. https://samoaglobalnews.com/your-attitude-will-determine-your-success-pm-to-rse-workers/.

Laslett, B., & Brenner, J. (1989). Gender and Social Reproduction: Historical Perspectives. *Annual Review of Sociology*, **15**, 381–404.

LeBaron, G., & Phillips, N. (2019). States and the Political Economy of Unfree Labour. *New Political Economy*, **24**(1), 1–21.

Lee, S., & Piper, N. (2017). Migrant Domestic Workers as 'Agents' of Development in Asia: An Institutional Analysis of Temporality. *European Journal of East Asian Studies*, **16**(2), 220–247.

Lemke, T. (2001). 'The Birth of Bio-politics': Michel Foucault's Lecture at the Collège de France on Neo-liberal Governmentality. *Economy and Society*, **30** (2), 190–207.

Lenard, P. (2021). Restricting Emigration for Their Protection? Exit Controls and the Protection of (Women) Migrant Workers. *Migration Studies*, **10**(3), 510–527.

Levitt, P., & De La Dehesa, R. (2003). Transnational Migration and the Redefinition of the State: Variations and Explanations. *Ethnic and Racial Studies*, **26**(4), 587–611.

Lewis, W. A. (1954). Economic Development with Unlimited Supplies of Labour. *Manchester School of Economic and Social Studies*, **22**, 139–191.

Likou, L. L. (2 May 2017). L.M.A.P. Officially Launches Programme. *Samoa Observer*. www.samoaobserver.ws/category/samoa/24133.

Lindio-McGovern, L. (2013). *Globalization, Labor Export and Resistance: A Study of Filipino Migrant Domestic Workers in Global Cities*, London: Routledge.

Lynch, C. (2007). *Juki Girls, Good Girls: Gender and Cultural Politics in Sri Lanka's Global Garment Industry*, Ithaca, NY: ILR Press/Cornell University Press.

Massey, D. S. (1998). New Migrations, New Theories. In D. S. Massey, J. Arango, G. Hugo, *et al.*, eds., *Worlds in Motion: Understanding International Migration at the End of the Millennium*, New York: Oxford University Press, pp. 1–16.

Massey, D. S., Arango, J., Hugo, G., *et al.* (1993). Theories of International Migration: A Review and Appraisal. *Population and Development Review*, **19**(3), 431–466.

Matsas, R. (2008). The Global Forum on Migration and Development: A New Path for Global Governance?, 20.

McGann, N. (20 February 2013). The Opening of Burmese Borders: Impacts on Migration. www.migrationpolicy.org/article/opening-burmese-borders-impacts-migration.

Meleisea, M. (7 July 2023). We Want the Forest but Fear the Spirits: Labour Mobility Predicaments in Samoa, part one. *DevBlog*, Acton: Newstex. https://devpolicy.org/labour-mobility-predicaments-in-samoa-part-one-20230707/.

Merla, L., Kilkey, M., & Baldassar, L. (2020). Examining Transnational Care Circulation Trajectories within Immobilizing Regimes of Migration: Implications for Proximate Care. *Journal of Family Research*, **32**(3), 514–536. https://doi.org/10.20377/jfr-351.

Mezzadri, A. (2019). On the Value of Social Reproduction. *Radical Philosophy*, **2**(04), 33–41.

Mezzadri, A., Newman, S., & Stevano, S. (2022). Feminist Global Political Economies of Work and Social Reproduction. *Review of International Political Economy*, **29**(6), 1783–1803.

Ministry of Foreign Employment Promotion and Welfare. (2008). *National Labour Migration Policy for Sri Lanka*, Colombo: Ministry of Foreign Employment Promotion and Welfare.

Napier-Moore, R. (2017). *Protected or Put in Harm's Way? Bans and Restrictions on Women's Labour Migration in ASEAN Countries*, Bangkok: International Labour Organisation (ILO) and UN Women. www.ilo.org/wcmsp5/groups/public/–asia/–ro-bangkok/–sro-bangkok/documents/publication/wcms_555974.pdf.

Natter, K. (2024). The Il/liberal Paradox: Conceptualising Immigration Policy Trade-Offs across the Democracy/Autocracy Divide. *Journal of Ethnic and Migration Studies*, **50**(3), 680–701.

Ness, I. (2023). *Migration as Economic Imperialism: How International Labour Mobility Undermines Economic Development in Poor Countries*, Medford, OR: Polity Press.

Nishitani, M., Boese, M., & Lee, H. (2023). The Production of Precariousness and the Racialisation of Pacific Islanders in an Australian Horticultural Region. *Journal of Ethnic and Migration Studies*, **49**(15), 3900–3919.

Nogami, N. (2017). *ILO Guide to Myanmar Labour Law – International Labour Organization*, Myanmar: International Labour Organization.

Oishi, N. (2005). *Women in Motion: Globalization, State Policies, and Labor Migration in Asia*, Stanford, CA: Stanford University Press.

Ong, A. (2006). *Neoliberalism as Exception: Mutations in Citizenship and Sovereignty*, Durham: Duke University Press.

Onis, Z., & Senses, F. (2005). Rethinking the Emerging Post-Washington Consensus. *Development and Change*, **36**(2), 263–290.

Østergaard-Nielsen, E. (Ed.). (2003). *International Migration and Sending Countries: Perceptions, Policies, and Transnational Relations*, Basingstoke: Palgrave Macmillan.

Parreñas, R. S. (2001). *Servants of Globalization: Women, Migration and Domestic Work*, Stanford, CA: Stanford University Press.

Parreñas, R. S. (2005). *Children of Global Migration: Transnational Families and Gendered Woes*, Stanford, CA: Stanford University Press.

Parreñas, R. S. (2008). *The Force of Domesticity: Filipina Migrants and Globalization*, New York: New York University Press.

Parreñas, R. S. (2015). *Servants of Globalization: Migration and Domestic Work*, 2nd ed., Stanford, CA: Stanford University Press.

Parreñas, R. S. (2021). Discipline and Empower: The State Governance of Migrant Domestic Workers. *American Sociological Review*, **86**(6), 1043–1065.

Petras, J. (1983). Marxism and World-Historical Transformations. *Social Text*, **8** (8, Winter), 40.

Petrou, K., & Connell, J. (2023). *Pacific Islands Guestworkers in Australia: The New Blackbirds?*, Singapore: Springer Verlag.

Petrou, K., & Withers, M. (2024). 'Sometimes, Men Cannot Do What Women Can': Pacific Labour Mobility, Gender Norms and Social Reproduction. *Global Networks*, **24**(2).

Philippine Overseas Employment Agency (POEA). (2002). *OFW Deployment by Skill, Country and Sex for the Year 2002*, Manila, Philippines: Philippine Government. www.dmw.gov.ph/archives/ofwstat/depperskill/1992.pdf.

Phillips, N. (2009). Migration as Development Strategy? The New Political Economy of Dispossession and Inequality in the Americas. *Review of International Political Economy*, **16**(2), 231–259.

Pineda-Ofreneo, R. (1991). *The Philippines, Debt and Poverty*, Manila: Published by Oxfam in Association with the Freedom From Debt Coalition.

Piper, N., & Grugel, J. (2015). Global Migration Governance, Social Movements, and the Difficulties of Promoting Migrant Rights. In C.-U. Schierup, R. Munck, B. Likic-Brboric, & A. Neergaard, eds.,

Migration, Precarity, and Global Governance, Oxford: Oxford University Press, pp. 261–278.

Piper, N., Rosewarne, S., & Withers, M. (2017). Migrant Precarity in Asia: 'Networks of Labour Activism' for a Rights-Based Governance of Migration: Debate: Addressing Migrant Precarity in Asia. *Development and Change*, **48**(5), 1089–1110.

Polanco, G. (2016). Consent behind the Counter: Aspiring Citizens and Labour Control under Precarious (Im)migration Schemes. *Third World Quarterly*, **37** (8), 1332–1350.

Polanco, G. (2019). Competition between Labour-Sending States and the Branding of National Workforces. *International Migration*, **57**(4), 136–150.

Polanyi, K. (1977). The Economistic Fallacy. *Review* (Fernand Braudel Center), **1**(1, Summer) 9–18.

Prasad, N. (2003). Small Islands' Quest for Economic Development. *Asia Pacific Development Journal*, **10**(1), 47–67.

Pyysiäinen, J., Halpin, D., & Guilfoyle, A. (2017). Neoliberal Governance and 'Responsibilization' of Agents: Reassessing the Mechanisms of Responsibility-Shift in Neoliberal Discursive Environments. *Distinktion: Journal of Social Theory*, **18**(2), 215–235.

Raghuram, P. (2009). Which Migration, What Development? Unsettling the Edifice of Migration and Development. *Population, Space and Place*, **15**(2), 103–117.

Rahman, M. M. (2012). Bangladeshi Labour Migration to the Gulf States: Patterns of Recruitment and Processes. *Canadian Journal of Development Studies/Revue Canadienne d'études Du Développement*, **33**(2), 214–230.

Rajapaksa, M. (2005). Mahinda Chintana: Victory for Sri Lanka, Presidential Secretariat of Sri Lanka, Colombo.

Rankin, K. N. (2001). Governing Development: Neoliberalism, Microcredit, and Rational Economic Woman. *Economy and Society*, **30**(1), 18–37.

Ratha, D. (2007). *Leveraging Remittances for Development*, Washington DC: Migration Policy Institute.

Ratha, D., & Mohapatra, S. (2013). Migrant Remittances and Development. In G. Caprio, ed., *The Evidence and Impact of Financial Globalization*, Amsterdam: Elsevier, pp. 121–130.

Ravenstein, E. G. (1885). The Laws of Migration – I. *Journal of the Statistical Society*, **48**(2), 167–227.

Richardson Jr., J. M. (2004). Violent Conflict and the First Half Decade of Open Economy Policies in Sri Lanka: A Revisionist View. In D. Winslow, & M. D. Woost, eds., *Economy, Culture and Civil War in Sri Lanka*, Bloomington, IN: Indiana University Press, pp. 41–72.

Rist, G. (2019). *The History of Development: From Western Origins to Global Faith*. (P. Camiller, Trans.), 5th ed., London: Zed.

Rodrigo, C., & Jayatissa, R. A. (1989). Maximising Benefits from Labour Migration: Sri Lanka. In R. Amjad, ed., *To the Gulf and Back: Studies on the Economic Impact of Asian Labour Migration*, New Delhi: ILO, pp. 255–296.

Rodriguez, R. M. (2002). Migrant Heroes: Nationalism, Citizenship and the Politics of Filipino Migrant Labor. *Citizenship Studies*, **6**(3), 341–356.

Rodriguez, R. M. (2010). *Migrants for Export: How the Philippine State Brokers Labor to the World*, Minneapolis, MN: University of Minnesota Press.

Romina Guevarra, A. (2006). Managing 'Vulnerabilities' and 'Empowering' Migrant Filipina Workers: The Philippines' Overseas Employment Program. *Social Identities*, **12**(5), 523–541.

Root, R. (11 July 2023). Patients Feel the Pain as Sri Lankan Healthcare Falls Victim to Economic Crisis. www.thenewhumanitarian.org/news-feature/ 2023/07/11/patients-feel-pain-sri-lankan-healthcare-falls-victim-economic-crisis.

Rose, N., O'Malley, P., & Valverde, M. (2006). Governmentality. *Annual Review of Law and Social Science*, **2**(1), 83–104.

Rosewarne, S. (2012). Trading on Gender: The Perversity of Asian Labour Exports as an Economic Development Strategy. *Work Organisation, Labour and Globalisation*, **6**(1), 81–102. https://doi.org/10.13169/workorgalaboglob .6.1.0081.

Rother, S. (2022). The 'Gold Standard' for Labour Export? The Role of Civil Society in Shaping Multi-level Philippine Migration Policies. *Third World Quarterly*, **43**(7), 1607–1626.

Ruiz, N. G. (2008). *Managing Migration: Lessons from the Philippines* (No. 45131), Washington, DC: The World Bank.

Sadiq, K., & Tsourapas, G. (2021). The Postcolonial Migration State. *European Journal of International Relations*, **27**(3), 884–912.

Sakalasooriya, N. (2021). Regional Development Disparities in Sri Lanka. *Open Journal of Social Sciences*, **09**(07), 62–91.

Samoa Global News. (20 May 2019). First Liaison Officer Based in Australia Appointed – Samoa Global News. *Samoa Global News*. https://samoaglobal news.com/first-liaison-officer-based-in-australia-appointed/.

Samoa Global News. Changes Needed to Selection Process of Seasonal Workers. (22 June 2021). Samoa Global News. https://samoaglobalnews.com/changes-needed-to-selection-process-of-seasonal-workers-scheme/.

San Maw Aung. (13 September 2023). Junta Requires Workers Abroad to Send Money Home via Approved Banks. *Radio Free Asia*. www.rfa.org/english/ news/myanmar/worker-remittances-09132023092811.html.

Sarkar, M. (2017). Constrained Labour as Instituted Process: Transnational Contract Work and Circular Migration in Late Capitalism. *European Journal of Sociology*, **58**(1), 171–204.

Schneiders, B. (28 February 2022). Samoan Farmworkers Told by Government Official to Quit Unions. *Sydney Morning Herald*. www.smh.com.au/national/ samoan-farmworkers-told-to-quit-white-people-unions-20220224-p59zbo .html.

Scott, S., & Rye, J. F. (2023). The Mobility–Immobility Dynamic and the 'Fixing' of Migrants' Labour Power. *Critical Sociology*, 08969205231197341.

Semyonov, M., & Gorodzeisky, A. (2004). Occupational Destinations and Economic Mobility of Filipino Overseas Workers. *International Migration Review*, **38**(1), 5–25.

Seneviratne, W., Sumanadasa, D., Thilakarathna, A., & Senaratne, R. (2023). Bilateral Labour Agreements between Sri Lanka and Other Jurisdictions: A Critical Legal Analysis, Colombo: Centre for Migration Research and Development (CMRD).

Shah, N. M. (1991). Asian Women Workers in Kuwait. *International Migration Review*, **25**(3), 464–486.

Shah, N. M. (2013). Labour Migration from Asian to GCC Countries: Trends, Patterns and Policies. *Middle East Law and Governance*, **5**(1–2), 36–70.

Shankman, P. (1976). *Migration and Underdevelopment: The Case of Western Samoa*, Boulder, Colo: Westview Press.

Shivakoti, R., Henderson, S., & Withers, M. (2021). The Migration Ban Policy Cycle: A Comparative Analysis of Restrictions on the Emigration of Women Domestic Workers. *Comparative Migration Studies*, **9**(1), 36.

Shutes, I. (2021). Gender, Migration and the Inequalities of Care. In C. Mora, & N. Piper, eds., *The Palgrave Handbook of Gender and Migration*, Cham: Springer International, pp. 107–120.

Silvey, R. (2004). Transnational Migration and the Gender Politics of Scale: Indonesian Domestic Workers in Saudi Arabia. *Singapore Journal of Tropical Geography*, **25**(2), 141–155.

Skeldon, R. (2006). Interlinkages between Internal and International Migration and Development in the Asian Region. *Population, Space and Place*, **12**(1), 15–30.

SLBFE | Support for Self Employment. (n.d.). Retrieved January 15, 2024, from http://www.slbfe.lk.

Sri Lanka Bureau of Foreign Employment (SLBFE). (2012). Different Perspectives of Departure Details, Sri Lanka Bureau of Foreign Employment. www.slbfe.lk/ file.php?FID=54.

Sri Lanka Bureau of Foreign Employment (SLBFE). (2022). *Outward Labour Migration in Sri Lanka*, Colombo: Sri Lanka Bureau of Foreign Employment (SLBFE).

Strange, S. (1996). *The Retreat of the State: The Diffusion of Power in the World Economy*, New York: Cambridge University Press.

Teo, T.-A. (2024). Responsible Migrants: Rights-Claiming, Risks and Costs at the Shelter. *Journal of Ethnic and Migration Studies*, 1–20.

Testaverde, M., Moroz, H., & Dutta, P. (2020). *Labor Mobility as a Jobs Strategy for Myanmar*, Washington, DC: World Bank. https://doi.org/10.1596/33957.

Thiollet, H. (2024). Immigration Rentier States. *Journal of Ethnic and Migration Studies*, **50**(3), 657–679.

Tigno, J. V. (2000). The Philippine Overseas Employment Program: Public Policy Management from Marcos to Ramos. *PUBLIC POLICY*, **4**(2), 37–86.

Triandafyllidou, A. (2022). Decentering the Study of Migration Governance: A Radical View. *Geopolitics*, **27**(3), 811–825.

Triandafyllidou, A., Bivand Erdal, M., Marchetti, S., *et al.* (2024). Rethinking Migration Studies for 2050. *Journal of Immigrant & Refugee Studies*, **22**(1), 1–21.

Tronto, J. C. (1993). *Moral Boundaries: A Political Argument for an Ethic of Care*, New York: Routledge.

Truong, T.-D. (1996). Gender, International Migration and Social Reproduction: Implications for Theory, Policy, Research and Networking. *Asian and Pacific Migration Journal*, **5**(1), 27–52.

Tsujita, M. (2018). Labour Migration in and out of Samoa. *The Journal of Samoan Studies*, **8**, 64–68.

Tyner, J. A. (2004). *Made in the Philippines: Gendered Discourses and the Making of Migrants*, London: RoutledgeCurzon.

Tyner, J. A. (2010). *The Philippines: Mobilities, Identities, Globalization*, Routledge. https://doi.org/10.4324/9780203892411.

Waring, M. (1988). *If Women Counted: A New Feminist Economics*, San Francisco, CA: Harper & Row.

Weeraratne, B. (2016). Protecting the Welfare of Children and its Causal Effect on Limiting Mother's Labour Migration. *International Migration*, **54**(5), 59–75.

Weeraratne, B. (2018a). *Migration and Gender Outcomes: Analysis of Selected Policies in Sri Lanka*, Geneva: World Bank.

Weeraratne, B. (2018b). Sub Agents and Migrants: Dissecting their Relationship to Guide Regulation. www.ips.lk/talkingeconomics/2018/05/22/sub-agents-and-migrants-dissecting-their-relationship-to-guide-regulation/.

Weeraratne, B. (4 July 2022). Good Riddance to the FBR: What Next to Increase Migrant Remittances to Sri Lanka? www.ips.lk/talkingeconomics/2022/07/04/good-riddance-to-the-fbr-what-next-to-increase-migrant-remittances-to-sri-lanka/.

Weerasooriya, N. (2013). A Requiem for Rizana . . . *Daily Mirror*, Colombo.

Weijun, E. (11 January 2018). Myanmar Lifts Ban on Sending Workers to Malaysia. *Free Malaysia Today*. www.freemalaysiatoday.com/category/nation/2018/01/11/myanmar-lifts-ban-on-sending-workers-to-malaysia/.

Wickramasekara, P. (2011). *Circular Migration: A Triple Win or a Dead End?* Geneva: ILO.

Wickramasekara, P. (2015). Bilateral Agreements and Memoranda of Understanding on Migration of Low Skilled Workers: A Review. *SSRN Electronic Journal*. https://doi.org/10.2139/ssrn.2636289.

Wickramasekara, P. (2016). South Asian Gulf Migration to the Gulf: A Safety Valve or a Development Strategy? *Migration and Development*, **5**(1), 99–129.

Withers, M. (2019a). Decent Care for Migrant Households: Policy Alternatives to Sri Lanka's Family Background Report. *Social Politics: International Studies in Gender, State & Society*, **26**(3), 325–347.

Withers, M. (2019b). *Sri Lanka's Remittance Economy: A Multiscalar Analysis of Migration-Underdevelopment*, London: Routledge, Taylor & Francis Group.

Withers, M. (2019c). Temporary labour migration and underdevelopment in Sri Lanka: the limits of remittance capital. *Migration and Development*, **8**(3), 418–436.

Withers, M. (2022). *Rapid Analysis of Family Separation Issues and Responses in the PALM Scheme – Final Report*, Australian Government.

Withers, M. (2024). Depletion through Transnational Social Reproduction: Guestworker Migration and Uneven Development in the South Pacific. *Work in the Global Economy*, **4**(1), 30–51.

Withers, M., & Hill, E. (2023). Migration and Development, without Care? Locating Transnational Care Practices in the Migration-Development Debate. *Population, Space and Place*, **29**(3), e2648.

World Bank (Ed.). (1993). *The East Asian Miracle: Economic Growth and Public Policy*, New York: Oxford University Press.

World Bank. (2006). *Global Economic Prospects: Economic Implications of Remittances and Migration*, Washington, DC: World Bank.

World Bank. (2020). *COVID-19 Crisis through a Migration Lens* (Migration and Development Brief No. 32), Washington DC: World Bank.

World Bank. (2023). *World Development Indicators*, Washington, DC: World Bank.

Wu, J., & Kilby, P. (2023). The Precarity of Gender, Migration, and Locations: Case Studies from Bangladesh and Nepal. *Development in Practice*, **33**(2), 145–155.

Yahampath, S. (2013). Enough is Enough. *Ceylon Today*, Colombo.

Yeates, N. (2008). *Globalizing Care Economies and Migrant Workers: Explorations in Global Care Chains*, Houndmills, Basingstoke, Hampshire: New York, NY: Palgrave Macmillan.

Yeates, N. (2009). Production for Export: The Role of the State in the Development and Operation of Global Care Chains. *Population, Space and Place*, **15**(2), 175–187.

Yeoh, B. S. A. (2016). Migration and Gender Politics in Southeast Asia. *Migration, Mobility, & Displacement*, **2**(1). https://doi.org/10.18357/mmd21201615022.

Yeoh, B. S. A. (2019). Corporeal Geographies of Labor Migration in Asia. In K. Mitchell, R. Jones, & J. Fluri, *Handbook on Critical Geographies of Migration*, Edward Elgar, pp. 92–105.

Yeoh, B. S. A., Huang, S., & Gonzalez, J. (1999). Migrant Female Domestic Workers: Debating the Economic, Social and Political Impacts in Singapore. *International Migration Review*, **33**(1), 114–136.

Zhang, X., Yang, J., & Wang, S. (2011). China Has Reached the Lewis Turning Point. *China Economic Review*, **22**(4), 542–554.

Zin, S. (21 January 2022). Myanmar's 'Army' of Overseas Workers Join Fight Against Junta. *The Irrawaddy*. www.irrawaddy.com/news/burma/myanmars-army-of-overseas-workers-join-fight-against-junta.html.

Cambridge Elements ☰

Global Development Studies

Peter Ho
Zhejiang University

Peter Ho is Distinguished Professor at Zhejiang University and high-level National Expert of China. He has held or holds the position of, amongst others, Research Professor at the London School of Economics and Political Science and the School of Oriental and African Studies, Full Professor at Leiden University and Director of the Modern East Asia Research Centre, Full Professor at Groningen University and Director of the Centre for Development Studies. Ho is well-cited and published in leading journals of development, planning and area studies. He published numerous books, including with *Cambridge University Press, Oxford University Press*, and *Wiley-Blackwell*. Ho achieved the William Kapp Prize, China Rural Development Award, and European Research Council Consolidator Grant. He chairs the International Conference on Agriculture and Rural Development (www.icardc.org) and sits on the boards of Land Use Policy, Conservation and Society, China Rural Economics, Journal of Peasant Studies, and other journals.

Servaas Storm
Delft University of Technology

Servaas Storm is a Dutch economist who has published widely on issues of macroeconomics, development, income distribution & economic growth, finance, and climate change. He is a Senior Lecturer at Delft University of Technology. He obtained a PhD in Economics (in 1992) from Erasmus University Rotterdam and worked as consultant for the ILO and UNCTAD. His latest book, co-authored with C.W.M. Naastepad, is *Macroeconomics Beyond the NAIRU* (Harvard University Press, 2012) and was awarded with the 2013 Myrdal Prize of the European Association for Evolutionary Political Economy. Servaas Storm is one of the editors of *Development and Change* (2006-now) and a member of the Institute for New Economic Thinking's Working Group on the Political Economy of Distribution.

Advisory Board
Arun Agrawal, *University of Michigan*
Jun Borras, *International Institute of Social Studies*
Daniel Bromley, *University of Wisconsin-Madison*
Jane Carruthers, *University of South Africa*
You-tien Hsing, *University of California, Berkeley*
Tamara Jacka, *Australian National University*

About the Series
The Cambridge Elements on Global Development Studies publishes ground-breaking, novel works that move beyond existing theories and methodologies of development in order to consider social change in real times and real spaces.

Cambridge Elements ☰

Global Development Studies

Elements in the Series

Printed in the United States
by Baker & Taylor Publisher Services